Dragonfly

Insights

A Visionary Guide to Self-awareness, Transformation, and Inner Peace

Martha Reed, PhD

Your Meta-Physician Providing Insights for Life

Library of Congress Control Number: 2018954512

ISBN: 978-0-9977477-1-3

First Printing: October, 2018

Published by: 102nd Place, LLC
Scottsdale, AZ

Printed in the United States of America

Disclaimer

This book is designed to provide information, education, and inspiration to its readers. It is sold with the understanding that the author is not, by this writing, engaged in rendering medical, psychological, or other professional advice. **The information contained herein may not be suitable for you. You should consult with a competent professional where appropriate.**

While the author has used her best efforts in preparing this book, she makes no representations or warranties concerning the accuracy or completeness of the contents and specifically disclaims any implied warranties.

The author shall not be liable for any loss or damage either physical, psychological, emotional, legal, financial, commercial or otherwise, including but not limited to special, incidental, consequential, or other damages caused, or alleged to be caused, directly, or indirectly, by the information contained in this book. You are responsible for your choices, actions, and consequences.

Contact the author at www.InsightsForLife.center regarding questions or suggestions related to materials, to relay personal experiences in successfully using these or similar techniques, and to schedule the author for speaking engagements or to conduct workshops.

Dedication

To my clients, family, and friends who
continue to inspire me daily.

Love, Martha

Table of Contents

The Gift of Balance

Many of us are familiar with the "Butterfly Effect," a theory which posits that a single occurrence, no matter how small, can change the course of the universe. An example is a butterfly vibrating its wings in South America causes an invisible ripple, which in turn affects the weather in Central Park. Our memories, good or bad, are also vibrations. They affect us mentally, emotionally, physically, and spiritually, forever changing the course of our lives. Memories are our butterflies, but in our case the ripple effect flows inward rather than outward.

Sometimes these ripples, particularly the negative ones, cause us to become unbalanced. When we are not in balance it is difficult to move forward. There's a fear that each step we take might result in a fall. We get stuck and we stay stuck. But it doesn't have to be this way. We can learn to be in balance. We can learn to control the vibrations within our body, mind, and spirit. We can become like the dragonfly.

When a dragonfly has all four wings in balance and working in perfect harmony, it can move confidently in any direction it chooses. What we need is dragonfly insight. We need to learn to balance our four wings – physical, emotional, mental, and spiritual. My purpose in writing this book is to gift you the tools and techniques you need to gain a life of balance and harmony – to become like the dragonfly.

At the core of all matter lies energy and the human body is no different. The energy body, our chakras, is the key to health, vitality, and happiness. Emotional energy or vibration resonates with life experiences, personal and professional relationships, and belief systems. It becomes encoded in the cell tissues of our body. This is all well and good when the energy or vibration is at a high frequency, but what about when it isn't? What do we do when the coding has a bug or a virus? We have to nudge the "deformed" field into normalcy, and we do this through energy therapies.

There are many types of energy therapies, but I've found a simple few tend to work best with most of my clients – understanding chakric energy, the use of color vibrations to heal, the power of love languages, and homeopathy as an adjunct to traditional western medicine. I'll take you through each of these in great detail, and I encourage you to experiment until you find the unique combination that is right for you.

Dragonfly Insights is designed to empower you, to encourage you, and to motivate you to get unstuck and become the powerful and beautiful person you wish to be. When I speak about empowerment, I mean the ability to raise your inner strength, self-confidence, self-motivation, positive attitude, and courage on mental, psychological, philosophical, and spiritual levels. Empowerment is a way of developing your gifts and allowing your brightness to shine.

This book is about transformation – your transformation. It's about your dream and your belief in your ability to get there. It's a book about attaining the ideal level of balance in your life – about allowing yourself the freedom to fly in any direction you choose without fear of falling.

I know some parts of this book might make you uncomfortable. I'll be asking you to dig deep to gain clarity and accomplish the change that you want. Sometimes when you are the most uncomfortable, the most significant breakthroughs occur. When you stir things up, you become aware. Awareness is what plants the golden root in your heart that allows you to grow.

I've heard some people, mainly women, say they feel selfish for taking the time to work on their happiness and desires. Let me lay that myth to rest right now. You are selfish if you don't. You cannot give fully of yourself if your heart is not full. You cannot pass on true happiness if you are not happy.

You cannot release positive energy into the world if you are vibrating at a low frequency. It is okay to want what you want, to have desires. You can have it. You can be it. You can do it. It is not beyond you.

Thank you for coming with me on this journey. You can change your life to be what you desire to be. You can create the most amazing, powerful, and beautiful world for yourself and those around you. It is my honor to guide you to becoming the extraordinary being you were meant to be.

Martha Reed

My Story

I wasn't always comfortable with my spiritual energy and my ability to help others. For a very long time I denied it, even though I knew I could see and feel things that others could not.

As a young child, I would see a bearded man walking from one corner of my room to the other. Now and then he would walk to the edge of my bed, lean over, and look at me. I was absolutely terrified of this man. This happened time and time again. If I told my parents, they would pooh-pooh me and say it's only a shadow from the streetlight, or your eyes are blurry, or there's a storm and the wind is merely moving the curtains. No one believed me, so I didn't trust what I was seeing was real. Now that I'm in tune with my spiritual energy, I know that he was a guardian spirit.

Then there would be the times when I felt that something was about to happen. I would tell the others who were to be involved, but again they'd make fun of me and say, "Oh you're such a know it all. You think you know everything, but you don' know anything." Even when the information I provided turned out to be true, no one believed me.

I remember one time I was standing out in the front of our apartment talking with a friend. A car drove by and I looked at my friend and said, "That car is going to get into an accident." About 30 seconds later we heard a big crash. He looked at me in surprise and fear. "You are too weird for me. I'm out of here," and he walked away from me. We have not spoken since.

I started keeping things to myself rather than be laughed at and made fun of by friends and family. I was very shy and introverted and the mean things people said hurt me deeply. They made me feel worse and worse about myself, like there was something wrong with me.

Hiding what I knew didn't keep me from being intrigued by it. In high school I began to explore the gifts I'd had since birth. I read everything I could find about the emotional and mental aspects of feelings. I was obsessed with anything having to do with psychic ability. I went to readings, practiced meditation, and explored mysteries. All of it in secret because, you know, what I was doing was weird, wacky stuff to most people. I never went too far though, afraid of the things I might see. Still not totally convinced I was anything special. Actually, it was quite the opposite, I had no community, no mentors, no one who was like me. I felt there must be something wrong with me.

After high school, I went to work in Corporate America and began my college studies, not towards my dream of a degree in counseling, but one in business management. I was convinced by a college advisor that a degree in counseling would be a terrible idea. He said I wouldn't even be able to pay off my school loans with such a career. Crushed but obedient, I persevered, utterly unaware of the shift my life would take. Ironically, it was my family who eventually led me there.

I have a nephew whose parents, my brother and his wife, are addicts. More times than I can count they have lost everything, their home, their car, their welfare, their food stamps. The three of them would sleep in open garages under people's cars. They would bathe in public pools, and when they did have housing, use pool water to cook and flush their toilets since they couldn't afford to have the water turned on. I had no idea how they ate.

I was very concerned about my nephew. I couldn't relate to the way his family lived, but I could relate to being the child of an addict. It was far out of my comfort zone, playing into every fear I ever possessed. Fears such as not feeling safe, not feeling secure, and not having a steady and stable environment. But he had grown up this way and didn't know anything else. He was very attached to his parents in spite of their inability to care for him in a way I felt was appropriate.

My husband and I took him as often as we could

We even thought about adopting him, but he made it clear that wasn't what he wanted. Two things happened that spurred me to want to help in any way I could. On the nights that he did stay with us, it was readily apparent that he was deeply afraid of the dark. He would tell me about the faces and the things he saw that would come after him.

One night he came into our room in tears, he was so afraid. I walked him back to his bed and told him a story. I remembered when I had first seen my guardian wandering by my bed, before I realized he was there to protect me, I used to pull the covers up over my head and cover every inch of my body, sure that he couldn't hurt me if none of my body were exposed, especially my feet! I knew that it didn't work. I'd remained terrified. But I didn't want to tell my nephew he was wrong, that he didn't see anything as so many had told me. I tried a different tactic. I told my nephew that the trick to making the bad things go away was to stare right at them. I said they couldn't stand the sight of human eyes looking at them. "When you stare at these things they disappear. Tonight, when you lay in bed, I want you to focus on them, peeking over the covers if you must but stare right at them, don't even blink. Just stare, stare, stare. They'll fade right before your eyes." I thought I was just making something up to help him because he was terrified, although now I know there is truth in what I said. At two o'clock in the morning he woke me up ecstatic. "It worked! It worked! I did it, and they melted!"

At the time, I had no awareness of the concept of mind-over-matter, or the power of intention. What I did know at that moment was that my simple suggestion impacted my nephew in such a massive way that it empowered him. He gained confidence in his ability to make what he saw vanish. He was no longer afraid.

The second incident had him showing up on my doorstep one day asking for something that I couldn't afford to give him. "Well, why not?" he demanded. "My mom and dad say you are rich." I was aghast, although I could understand how he might believe that considering his upbringing. I wasn't anywhere near rich, in fact I was hard pressed to call myself middle-classed. All I could think was if this boy thought my lifestyle was only for the rich, then what hope was there for him to aspire to have more and be more. I wanted him to dream bigger, bigger than what I had. I wanted somehow to help him get past those small beliefs.

About the same time that my concerns for my nephew's well-being were escalating, my mother came by. She wanted me to take her to a hypnotherapy appointment. I didn't even know these people existed. I thought hypnotherapy was only in the movies or a magic trick, where they took over your mind, made you quack like a duck, or stole your money. I just looked at her like she was crazy. She said, "Stop looking at me like that. I've done this before and it really works." So, I took her, and while I was waiting for her session to finish a thought came to me. If this works for her, I wonder if this would work for my nephew.

I spoke to the hypnotherapist afterwards about helping my nephew. She said he would need multiple sessions, and they were expensive. At least not a part of my budget at the time, since I was in my early thirties, had just had a baby, and was not making much at my corporate job. But as we know, the universe works in mysterious ways. The next day, as grace would have it, I saw an advertisement in a magazine for hypnotherapy training. The cost of this class was the same as the cost of the sessions. I knew if I could learn to be a hypnotherapist, I would be able to help my nephew for the rest of his life without having to worry about paying for additional sessions.

I was floating on cloud nine, but my husband was not and was against me taking the class. He thought it was a waste of money and I was being scammed. He hadn't quite come on board yet with the idea that we have the power within ourselves to make major changes. But I had a strong pull toward this class. I knew I had to take it and I did. It was 2002 – the beginning of my dragonfly transformation.

Learning hypnotherapy did allow me to give my nephew the help he needed. But it did so much more than that. From the first day of class, it became crystal clear that this was something I was destined to do. I was gifted at it, it came naturally to me, and I loved it. At the time I was still working at my office job, so I began seeing clients in my home in the evenings. Once my husband started to see how I was truly able to help people he became more open to what I was doing. But it wasn't until I worked with him to gain the confidence he needed to be accepted into the fire department, that he totally believed in me.

As time went on I realized I was no longer happy working at my corporate job. All day I would think of nothing but getting home and working with my clients. Working out of my home, however, was beginning to be a problem. It wasn't fair to my family, asking them to be quiet when a client was visiting and always having to keep the house clean. As soon as I felt I could support myself doing the work I loved, I quit my job.

It wasn't the best timing – 2008 when the recession hit. I'd moved my practice to a chiropractic center. My new hours were 9 to 5, Monday through Friday at this center. It hadn't occurred to me at the time, there was a reason that clients saw me in the evenings and on weekends. Their schedules didn't allow for daytime appointments. Also, with the recession strapping everyone, hypnotherapy became a luxury that even some of my clients who had seen significant improvements felt they could no longer afford.

On top of that, the bank pulled my credit line.

thought for sure I was going to land flat on my face and lose everything. I knew I was going to hear it from everybody that it was the worst mistake of my life and I shouldn't have done it. I was devastated trying to figure out what I was going to do.

Again, the universe, God, Spirit, or whatever you believe, intervened. My dog had a torn meniscus and I had just found out it would cost $2,500 to have it fixed. I didn't have that kind of money. But I wanted to help my dog so I began researching alternatives and finding nothing. Feeling defeated, I took a break and went out back and read a novel. Out of nowhere, in large print, the words "homeopathic wellness" appeared before my eyes. These words weren't even in the book and I'd never heard the word homeopathic before. By this time, though, I'd learned to trust my instincts when these things happened. So, I went to the internet and searched for homeopathic. The first article I read was talking about healing yourself naturally from various ailments, one of them being problems with the knees. I figured if it could work for humans it could probably work with dogs. This was my first formal introduction to energy as medicine, yet it felt so familiar and right.

That night I was reading the paper and saw an Acute Symptom and First Aid Homeopathic course was starting in a few days. Again, I had that knowing. I ended up attended the American College of Homeopathic Medicine and went on to study metaphysics. Years later I earned a PhD in holistic life counseling from the University of Sedona.

All this time I was still trying to build my practice but was having stronger and stronger intuition that the chiropractic center didn't have the right energy. All of my study, and the messages from my body energy, were telling me I needed to move if I truly wanted to be my highest and best self. In 2010 I left and opened my Insights for Life center. It's been full steam ahead ever since. Onward and upward!

Dragonfly Insights

I'm sure by now some of you are wondering about the dragonfly and how it came to be a metaphor for allowing individuals to emerge and discover their true purpose and happiness. Let me tell you. I had moved into my own space but was having difficulty determining what my real purpose was, who exactly was I meant to serve? I had learned all these various modalities that could help hundreds of different people – hypnotherapy, life coaching, spiritual counseling, reiki, color therapy, etc. – but knew in my heart that I needed to narrow my focus.

One night, in a dream, a dragonfly appeared to me. The dragonfly knew that I believed a whole-person approach, combining mind, body, and spirit, was the only way to heal physically, mentally, emotionally, and spiritually. It flew close and said it was capable of flying in any direction it chose if every one of its wings were working in perfect harmony and in perfect balance. If one of its wings was slightly out of balance or out of calibration, it could still get to where it wanted to go but not without a struggle. It wouldn't get there with ease and grace.

If, however, one of its wings was missing or broken, it wouldn't get there at all. The best it could do would be to spin in circles going nowhere. It might become functionally dependent on the help of other dragonflies or maybe just completely give up and die. "The same is true for you," it said.

At that moment I knew it was a powerful message. The dragonfly wings represent the mental, the emotional, the physical, and the spiritual aspects of life. We too can fly in any direction we choose if each of our elements is working in perfect balance and harmony. When they aren't, we get stuck. We spin our wheels, getting nowhere, sometimes out of control, spiraling further and further down.

The dragonfly began to appear to me more frequently. It would show me visions of what it was like to have an injured wing, how hard it was and how much energy had to be put into getting from point A to point B. It was trying to make it clear to me that life is not easy if you are wounded, but it's not impossible either. One night it came to me and said, "There are butterfly people and dragonfly people, who will you serve?"

I knew that butterflies were supposed to represent transformation, but let's think about them. The mother lays her eggs on tender, little soft leaves so when the caterpillar is born it has everything it needs to survive and succeed in its quest to become a butterfly. Many people are caterpillars. They hop grazing from leaf to leaf. Then one day they realize they do not like their life, and decide they want something bigger and better. They become a beautiful butterfly. That's not to say that bad things don't happen to caterpillars, they might be eaten by birds, or poisoned by pesticides, but the foundation is laid for them from the beginning to be successful.

Contrast that to the dragonfly. The mother lays her eggs in the dark, murky water of marshes and streams where they may, or may not, attach to a plant. Once they hatch they must scour for their food: tiny tadpoles or fish. No easy meal, like being born on top of your lunch bucket. They have to learn to survive in very rough, dark situations. They have to suck air in and out of their rectums to be able to move. It takes a lot for them to get from one place to another in life.

Like caterpillars that become butterflies, dragonfly babies are called nymphs and don't look anything like a dragonfly while they are underwater. Unlike caterpillars though, the nymphs may choose when they want to emerge from the dark, dank waters into the light above. For some it may be only a matter of a few months, for others it could be as long as five years.

Once they decide, they find a reed or a stick and travel up and into the light. There they'll attach to a plant and wait for their shell to dry and crack so the dragonfly they were meant to be can emerge

When it does, it immediately takes flight, hovering over the water balancing his or her reflection.

The dragonfly no longer thinks about when they used to be stuck in the dark. The ones that are stuck in the past are still there. Once they decide and emerge, they know there is no going back. All they can do is wait for the others to join them in the light. It can be lonely.

The dragonfly said, "Your people are dragonfly people. They are hurting, but when they come to you it's because they have decided it's time to emerge." I knew instantly the dragonfly was right. Is it simply a coincidence that my last name happens to be Reed? Dragonfly became not only a metaphor for the work I would do, but also my personal animal totem.

Dragonflies as Animal Totems

What does it mean to relate to a dragonfly as an animal totem? If you've not heard the word before, totems are sometimes called spirits. Every animal has a spirit that is made up of their talents, abilities, gifts, teachings, and spiritual powers. It is part of their inner nature to want to communicate messages about these things to the human world.

Your spirit animal is an embodiment of your mind, body, and spirit, and therefore cannot be chosen. It must choose you, as the dragonfly chose me. To recognize your animal spirit, pay close attention. It may come to you in a dream, while you are meditating, or even in physical form in everyday life, like seeing pictures of a hawk everywhere you go. Look for a repetitive pattern, at least three times in a short period. You must develop a continual relationship with them so they can teach or guide you. Their spirits must be respected and honored so they may pass those energies and talents to you. Generally, there is one power animal that will stay with you throughout your life. However, additional animal spirits may come and go for various periods of time depending on the assistance you seek.

Insects as totems are ancient and primitive and can be potent allies because of their primal and direct connection to Spirit. Insects have a connection to all the realms of nature – land, air, and water – as they can crawl, fly, and swim. Dragonflies can do all of these and are very powerful animal spirits. Insects are adaptable and can represent protection due to their exoskeleton, and the ability to make life changes because of their metamorphosis. They are explorers, opportunists, and survivalists. Dragonflies, in particular, exhibit these qualities.

As an animal totem, the dragonfly teaches its talents and spiritual powers in many ways. A person with the dragonfly as a totem will not need to struggle to learn its lessons since the dragonfly is a gentle teacher. If this spirit animal appears in your life, you are being called to transform and evolve

Its spirit brings the inspiration to invoke changes that are required to reach your full potential. The dragonfly is constantly changing and reinventing itself, and it is important to remain open to the progress of your journey. The dragonfly's emergence is about reinventing yourself, making changes within, and not letting your past or your habits control who you are, or who you become. It is a true awakening of the inner spirit.

People with the dragonfly as a totem may begin life as very emotional, but as they grow they gain more balance and mental clarity. The dragonfly's lesson is to merge water and air. Water represents emotions and subconscious mind and air represents the thoughts and the conscious mind. Regardless of whether or not the dragonfly is your lifelong totem, when you unite these two sides, you receive the dragonfly's gifts. You become your own dragonfly.

Spiritual Beings

All living things are spiritual beings, including humans. You may have heard the saying we are all spiritual beings having a human experience. It is true. Our spirits have chosen to take on a human form to either learn a lesson that will bring us to higher energy or vibration or help others to attain higher energy.

When I was growing up, I felt everything in everyone. I would later discover the word for this is an empath. It is the root of the word empathy, the ability to understand and share the feelings of another. Often, we experience empathy with others if we've shared some type of similar experience. A true empath, however, does not need to have experienced what another is going through. I believe that we are all true empaths to one degree or another depending on our vibrational levels.

The problem with being emphatic and not knowing it, is that we unwittingly take on and identify with things and feelings that belong to other people. We think they are our own. We do not always have the ability to decipher between the problems, feelings, and mental states of others and those that belong to us. This is because on a higher level there is no difference between what is yours and what is mine. It is all energy – shared energy.

When I was little, I could sense a Light in people. It was a golden light, like a seed. Through no fault of his own, as the result of an accident, my dad became addicted to pain medications. I would ask him to stop taking them and he would say, "The doctor told me to take the pills. I have to take them." Like most addicted to something, as the dosage became less and less effective, he began to take way more than the doctors ever prescribed. His generation didn't question a doctor's judgement. Responsibility for decisions about their health was the doctor's job, and their job was to follow "doctor's orders."

Even so, I could still sense this seed of golden light in him. When he wasn't on his medication, it was as if he was the best dad ever. I could see his truth and I just loved him. He and I were very close. I was daddy's little girl. When he took his medication, he was mean. I would see him literally step out of his body. He transitioned into something else. In the Light he was functioning from his spiritual side, but medication had him functioning from his physical side.

My dad is not alone. We all have both a spiritual and a physical side. Like him, we often get caught up and stuck in our physical side because it is difficult to remember when we were purely spiritual beings. To transform like the dragonfly, we need to play more and work with our spiritual side. When my dad was in the muck, it was ugly. But when he was in the Light, it was awesome. Having this experience with my dad, has helped me to understand and be able to help others come into the Light and stay there. I am grateful for everything I have been through because I know the accumulation of my experiences are the very things that are creating the uniqueness called Me.

When you are down and depressed, not happy, and living in the shadows or in darkness, that is when you are much more in your physical side. Maybe you have temporarily forgotten about your light and spiritual side. As the old saying goes, "seeing is believing." This is why we more easily believe that the physical side is the truth. In many ways it is, but it is not the whole truth.

Everything that you have been through, whether it was right, wrong, good, bad, or indifferent, is part of who you are. Not one of those things needs to define who you will be tomorrow. Who you are is so much more than what you've lived through. You are a vast, spiritual, powerful, and beautiful being. Know that you are not broken because of your experiences or circumstances. Some of us may be more bent than others. Sometimes it takes a really big hammer to bang out all those dings and bends to get things straight. Bent is not broken. Ben simply means you are not how you want to be or how you would choose to be. Awareness of being bent is your cue to begin your journey up the reed and into the Light.

Both the physical and the spiritual sides of each of us have a vibration. The physical side is slower moving, dense, and heavy. It forgets that it has the power to speed up and become the Light. The spiritual side is weightless and moves fast. It sometimes escapes our attention because it is so rapid, and we forget about it. The spiritual side is carefree and happy. It is a vibration that is infectious, affecting everyone around you.

While it is possible, although not desirable, to remain in your physical side indefinitely, you cannot stay at a high spiritual vibration for long. Your physical and mental states would be completely drained in a few hours. We have chosen to place our spirits into a physical form so we must bring our energy, our vibration, back to neutral at some point in order to survive.

Self-Check Exercise

Now would be a good time to check in with your energy. Close your eyes and take notice ... how do you feel right now? What's your current vibration?

Energy and Vibration

Go to any rock concert and you'll find gigantic speakers. The manufacturers know that the music has to vibrate at a specific frequency for the ear to hear. The deep bass vibrates at a lower frequency that you can feel in the body. I feel it in my chest area the most.

There are many different frequencies and levels of vibration within our emotions as well. There is an anger frequency. There is a melancholy frequency. There is an arousal frequency. Each frequency is a form of energy. Just like a radio dial, what we tune into is what we get. If you tune into a classical station, you will get classical music, you won't get rock 'n' roll.

If you are standing in a room you can sense when somebody comes in or somebody is coming up behind you, or something is going on. When you are in tune, your awareness is on alert, you can feel it. You can feel that sense. The same is true if you are standing in front of someone. You have the ability to project yourself at them. You can project your mood or your emotions onto them which in turn may affect their energy.

We have the ability to send and we have the ability to receive. It goes both ways. These energy centers spin in funnel fashion. That means we don't receive information in a straight line and we don't send it in a straight line. Everything is a spiral, starting out wider and getting stronger in frequency as it funnels in or funnels out.

This is one reason it is so important to surround yourself with people who exude positive energy. Have you heard the sayings, you're only as good as the company you keep, or you're only as good as your five closest friends? It is extremely difficult for you to vibrate at a high frequency and emerge as an extraordinary being if you surround yourself with low frequency vibrations. If your friends are negative, always complaining, or in constant crisis, their lack of energy will bring you down. Remember I said we are all empaths whether we are conscious of it or not. You will empathically pick up on their frequencies, and if you aren't aware, you may mistake them for your own. If you've ever felt sad or blue or stressed for no apparent reason, your spirit is likely taking on low frequencies from someone in your life.

It is possible to feel or experience what the others we are energetically connected to are feeling. Sometimes I'd get sick. My head would hurt. I'd get a pain in my back. My nose would run. I'd stop myself and ask, "Am I really sick? What is really going on? How do I really feel?" I then review everything I am feeling physically, then emotionally and mentally. This is called awareness talk. I simply describe exactly what is going on in an objective way.

Then I ask, "Is this mine? Am I truly getting sick?" If it is mine, I explain to my immune system what we need to do. Sometimes the answer will come as a picture of another being such as one of my children, or even my dog. I may ask, "Who does this belong to?" I don't always get an answer. When I make the connection that it is not mine, it goes away rapidly, within a minute or two.

It works the same with emotions. If I'm in a bad mood and I don't know why, then I'm fairly certain the feeling is not mine. I can instantly shift and say, "I don't know who this belongs to, but I have absolutely no reason to feel bad today." I do not judge the feelings or blame them on anything like hormones or circumstances. If you take away all blame and excuses for the feelings and ask, "Do I really have a reason to feel this way?" the majority of the time the answer is going to be no. When that is the case, the feeling belongs to somebody else. That person is an energy vampire who has tapped into you.

There is something you can do to oust the vampire. It's a visualization exercise I call Return to Sender.

Return to Sender Exercise

Close your eyes. Scan your body and ask yourself, how am I feeling right now? Then ask yourself if this is how you want to feel. If something feels off or you are not feeling like you want to feel, it may not be your energy. Imagine you are feeling something in your emotional body you know you have no reason to feel such as anger, sadness, fatigue, jealousy, etc. Imagine that you take an air blower or a fan and place it above your head. Say to yourself, "Whoever this belongs to, I no longer choose to feel this way for you. I return this to sender." As you say it, imagine that the wind from the blower blows down on the top of your head and pushes everything that is within you out of you; everything that does not belong to you. Blow it all off of you. Imagine it leaving your body. See it flying out and away and returning to the sender.

> RETURN TO SENDER

Who it belongs explicitly to is of no concern. It makes no difference if it is from the stranger who called yelling at you, or from your brother, your child, your boss, or a coworker. It doesn't matter. It could be from each of them. They all get blown off. Blow it all away completely and return it to sender. When you feel every last speck is out of your being you can open your eyes.

When we do this, we take our power back and get rid of those feelings that belong to someone else. It is amazing how much better we feel. It helps bring us into a feeling of peace because we own our space. You can use Return to Sender at any time. You do not need to have a specific feeling or thought in mind. You can do it in general and return anything that belongs to someone else without knowing consciously what or whose it is.

Words as Energy

What people say also has energy. In fact, words hold tremendous power over your energy if you allow them. When you hear someone say something, their words can create a new thought for you that may change how you are feeling. This can work in positive or negative ways.

It is also why talking to the right person at the right time can be the perfect thing, like when you react with, "That's exactly what I needed to hear." Or maybe someone says something encouraging, motivational, or even completely random, and it changes your entire day.

Words can work in negative ways too, and it may seem at times in your life where this is the norm rather than the exception. You may have been listening to someone on the phone who was in a negative space. Even though that person may be thousands of miles away, his energy can still affect you. His conversation and his energy are simultaneously transferred all the way through the air, into the ethers, and down and about where it settles into your ear. Some of this negative energy manages to get into your head and form a little, tiny thought. From there it can plant a seed. That seed of negativity might grow until it gets so large it needs to find a way to escape. It could come out in the form of words. You can easily pass it along to other people. You can just as easily pass it back into the phone all the way across the world and back into the caller's ear.

There are satellites, transmission towers and technologies that unknowingly transfer this negative energy. It is like magic. We don't see the energy traveling through the air because it is invisible. How many conversations are in the air right now? How many cell phones, radios, wireless devices, thoughts, undercurrents, messages, and signals are being broadcast every second? Every one is a frequency that we can tune into and they are everywhere.

Back to the negative caller. What if they were a loved one calling and you were caught off guard, not knowing how they were feeling? Maybe you weren't having the best day and weren't in the best place emotionally either. Then the negative energy they were transmitting could have a significant affect on you if you choose to let it. You could allow it to bring you down, make you angry, or upset you. You could choose to start feeling the way they do. Or, you could choose to become aware of the negative energy and use it to bring your energy level up, allowing it to launch you forward to a way you would rather feel.

What if you did not know who the caller was and had no idea what they were talking or yelling about? What if it was a wrong number? Then the negative energy may not affect you at all. Or if it does, it might be short-lived since you are not emotionally attached or invested in the caller. Or maybe you will choose to be mad all day over it. Whatever it is, or whoever is calling, you can always take a quick moment to pause and decide how you want to be feeling. Remember it is just a frequency and you can tune it in or you can tune it out. You can easily reflect on a positive experience you've recently had, or something for which you're grateful. Take a breath and focus on that positive feeling.

Let's say right before the call came in you had just found out you got the job you were hoping for. You'd been unemployed for two years and finally you'll have money again. In this case the crazy, negative caller couldn't possibly bring you down or steal your thunder because you are on too big of a high, too high of a cloud. Your vibration is at a high level too, and the low level of the caller's vibration cannot meet yours. It is impossible to resonate with their low frequency. This makes it easy to detach and let it go.

Everything is about frequency and how we resonate with different frequencies. That being said, I don't believe we have to be terribly strict with which words we use all the time. To do so would make us crazy and cause too much stress. We can, however, learn to use words that vibrate at a frequency that is not harmful to us or others. And while it is important to gain more control over our words, there are times when what we have to say is precisely what we need to say. We can edit our words to a certain degree and use words to our advantage, but self-expression is important.

Words have the power to create. What you say can cause changes in your attitude, actions, and feelings. Words can also give the command to your subconscious to create the desired outcome. Words give energy. There is an entire area of scientific study known as Neural Linguistic Programming, or NLP, which has proven the power of words in helping individuals to transform their lives.

Words can be used to cause instant changes in one's psyche. Strong emotional words in a song or poem can bring instant deep feelings. They can make you laugh, cry, feel sorrow, feel tired, or energize you.

Reframing your words and speech patterns can work miracles in your life. There are simple ways to change negative words into positive ones to help create the life you want. For example:

A "problem" can become a "challenge."
A "challenge" can become an "opportunity."

You could even say, "I have a challenge that many people would say is very bad, but I am working on creating an opportunity. It will be fun to see how it all works out."

When something "makes you really mad," you could say, "this isn't my ideal situation."

If "you can't," maybe change to "it's because you haven't learned how to, yet."

Change "I am trying" to "I am doing" or "I am bringing about" or "I am manifesting."

Change "I might be able to do that" to "I can do it" or "I will do it." Might is a word that designates non-commitment.

Instead of saying "This is hard," you could say "This is not as easy as I anticipated but I am getting better at it."

The words "please" and "thank you" are always powerful. These are very positive words. They are for more than just being polite. There's a reason they are called "the magic words."

Spiritual Beings as Energy

Some people can have stronger effects on our energy than others. This is especially true with family members. We have biological connections to our families that tend to cause the energetic connections to be powerful. I have seen many clients who were in a very positive space and then after a visit to their family, or even one particular family member, they become drained or pulled back into a very negative space. I have worked with many mothers whose children seem to have incredible power over them. They had let their children have inappropriate influence over them, until we found ways they could use to take their power back. Then they were able to change their relationships with their children into something positive for everyone.

We are all energetically connected on some level, but when we have some concrete meeting or any kind of association between us, the connection is much stronger. We become corded together. Our energies, instincts, and emotions become part of this connection. I am energetically connected to each of my clients and our connection is strong because I have worked with them face-to-face. I am connected with each of you because we have a link through this book. I know I am connected to your frequency in some way, even if neither of us can feel it.

As an empath and intuitive, I connect with people without even trying. Right now, I'm tapping into you on some level because I want to know the best way to write so I can reach you and help you gain the most benefit from this material. I do this not only to serve, but to understand others. I believe we all do this on a subconscious level. We naturally want to communicate, connect, and understand others. Everything we have ever experienced gives us lots of frequencies to attune to.

When a person throws us off balance and out of our ideal frequency it is our job to know how to recover and to understand that they just knocked us off center. The chapter on chakras will teach you techniques for recovery and how to deal with frequencies that knock you off center.

Environment as Energy

There are people around our environment who affect our well-being. Everyone knows negative people. Everyone knows dream stealers. Everyone knows energy vampires. These are people who drain your energy. People who make us feel worn down when we are around them. These are the people who knock us off balance on many levels. Sometimes it might be on one level, such as mentally. Sometimes it may be on an emotional level, and other times it may be physical. Or it can be a combination of all three.

If you live in a lousy environment, if you don't resonate with it, it is not going to resonate in you. This can include your home life, your job, the car you drive, your community, the people around you, your neighborhood, and even the city or country in which you live. This is why exploring and trying different things is so important. It helps us to become exposed to different frequencies and we can test how we resonate. Travel, meet new people, join different social circles and groups, and keep seeking. Even driving a different route to work can have an enormous effect.

When the dragonfly is ready to move to a new environment it undergoes a wonderful and beautiful transformation, one that is not always easy, but always for the highest good. After emerging the dragonfly is more colorful and beautiful, and both it, and its environment benefit from its change.

It is okay not to know exactly where you fit in. Everything is always changing naturally. We can make our own changes too. We can find ourselves in a situation or environment that seems almost ideal. When we get there, we can begin to make changes that bring it even closer to what we really want. We can keep fine tuning it and adjust ourselves so we can make it better and better. This is just like the dragonfly making changes to its skin colors. They keep changing throughout its life, they do not stay the same. And your true colors will change too!

Chakras

We've talked about different forms of energy, but how do we, as spiritual beings having a human experience, hold energy? We hold it inside our chakras. In Eastern medicine, chakras are whorls or vortices of energy located within the etheric body. These chakras start at the base of the spine and follow up the spine to the top of the head. There are seven primary chakras – the root, the sacral, the solar plexus, the heart, the throat, the third eye, and the crown.

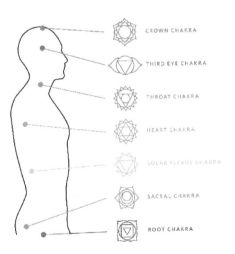

CROWN CHAKRA

THIRD EYE CHAKRA

THROAT CHAKRA

HEART CHAKRA

SOLAR PLEXUS CHAKRA

SACRAL CHAKRA

ROOT CHAKRA

Chakras are simply different aspects of consciousness. Any imbalance in consciousness plays out in the chakras and could lead to an imbalance in hormones secreted by the endocrine glands. The endocrine system regulates body functions through the production of hormones. If any aspect of consciousness is out of balance for too long, physical dis-ease may appear.

An imbalance may manifest itself in two ways. One, you could have a low energy imbalance. This means that you don't have enough energy in that chakra and so you experience insufficiencies or a sense of lacking. The other is that you may have more energy in the chakra than you need. This may cause over-reactions or symptoms of excess in both physical and emotional areas. The use of color to correct imbalance on both ends of the spectrum can be very effective.

These energy centers are sending and receiving all the time. They each have their own frequency. The lower the chakra, the denser it is and the slower it moves. The higher the chakra the closer it gets into your spiritual side, your Akashic Records, your soul, your higher-self, your connection to Source, Angels, Guides, or whatever you prefer to call it. We are connected to all levels of reality – above and below. All levels are within us and move through us, dovetailing in a beautiful and colorful way.

Holistic chakra balancing can improve well-being on all levels: mental, emotional, physical, and spiritual. Getting our chakras in balance and maintaining that balance, is the key to improving health and eliminating or avoiding chronic conditions altogether. Specific chakra therapies will be required depending on the type of imbalance you are experiencing.

Chakra Ages

Each of your chakras is associated with an age in which it develops. The ages, like the chakras, occur in sets of seven. The number seven has special significance. It is the number of perfection, security, safety, and rest. It combines the number three of the heavens and the soul with the number four of the earth and the body. Therefore, it finds a place between the two worlds. It represents the spiritual maturity we acquire after a learning cycle. This is why the seventh chakra – the crown – represents enlightenment.

The Root, the most basic of the chakras, develops between birth and seven (0-7) years-old. Think about what happens during this time. You are being born which is a major event. Safety and security are shaky. It is very easy for imbalance to occur. A person at this age is vulnerable and susceptible to the influences of conditioning, food additives, vaccines, and other chemicals. Healthy nutrition, nourishment, and loving care are critical.

The Sacral develops between ages seven to fourteen

(7-14). Education and social integration begin around this time. Exploration and identity develop.

The Solar Plexus develops between the ages of fourteen to twenty-one (14-21). Emotional development and integration occur. Romantic activity and personal independence increase. Here, health issues need to be kept in balance. It's easy to be "set off" by something trivial and even easier to be knocked completely off-balance by a significant event such as a car accident.

The Heart develops between the ages of twenty-one to twenty-eight (21-28). These are the years of career and/or family building. This is another important time of personal development. Stress from one's work environment or bad relationships can cause great imbalance.

The Throat develops between twenty-eight to thirty-five (28-35). Usually a time of personal journeys and transformation.

The Third Eye develops between thirty-five to forty-two (35-42). Spiritual maturity and wisdom occur during this time along with the ability to teach.

The Crown finally comes into being between forty-two and forty-nine (42-49). Enlightenment and a higher awareness are possible, as is a general rebirth.

This is not to say that these chakras or energy

centers are not always with you and active regardless of your age. They are. If they were not, then you would be dead or dying. Even at seven-years-old you still have every chakra functioning. Each is absorbing, learning, taking on cellular memories, and taking on imprints in anticipation of when it will come to maturity. From birth to seven for example you are learning foundational things such as support, security, passion, and drive. That is why we talk about how important it is to have a good foundation.

The maturity of a chakra does not mean you will not experience an imbalance in that chakra later in life. Imbalances may occur at an early age but not fully manifest until you are older and more aware. It is the awareness of an imbalance that allows you to make the self-correction necessary to bring it back to normalcy.

Let's begin to explore each of the chakras in more detail. There are colors associated with each chakra as well. As mentioned earlier, color is a specific therapy that can be used to correct an imbalance. I have found it to be such an effective medium that I have devoted an entire chapter to it.

The Root Chakra (Birth to 7)
Color: Red
Endocrine Gland: Gonads and adrenal medulla
Function: Fight or Flight response

Issues: Foundation, self-preservation, survival instincts, grounding

The Root chakra is the lowest of the primary chakras. It is located at the base of the spine. It is appropriately named root, as its main focus is to keep us "grounded" to the earth and the physical plane. The Root chakra is the vortex where the energetic body's primary concern is survival and meeting the physical body's needs. The Root chakra brings up issues of self-preservation, the right to exist, and to stand up for oneself – to be rooted in the earth and to hold a rightful place. Your desire to eat, have shelter and protection are all part of the Root chakra. Remember the Root chakra is developed between birth and seven-years-old. During this period, the infant or young child can only think of herself and her own basic needs.

When you honor who you really are and accept others for who they are, you have the foundation for a strong Root chakra. Affirming yourself will allow you to make positive choices for your well-being and open yourself to what life has to offer. A person with a healthy, balanced Root chakra is secure with his place on earth, has a high sense of security that he can provide for himself, and is well-grounded to the events that surround his life. Some characteristics of a balanced Root chakra include courage, determination, assertiveness, good health, and stability.

An imbalance in the Root chakra is indicated by feelings of insufficiency or a sense of lacking. An imbalance can result in feelings of insecurity, not being grounded, and not belonging. You may feel that the world is unsafe, and you may be unsure of your place within it. Beliefs about yourself and others may limit your life choices or cause you to overreact.

An imbalance in the Root chakra may also be indicative of a higher than normal level of energy. This excessive energy may lead you to do things such as overeat, be afraid of change, have an addiction to feeling secure, become aggressive, or become overly greedy.

In addition to the color therapy that I will discuss in the next chapter, there are affirmations that you can say to help you bring your chakras back into balance. They must be said with conviction and a true believing for your subconscious mind to internalize them. Here are some you may want to try with an unbalanced Root chakra.

I will

repeat these

daily!

- I have all the talents and abilities I need to manage my life's tasks.

- I have all the talents and skills I need to fulfill my life's purpose.
- I direct my impulses toward my life goals and I will persevere.
- I focus on my goal in life, and I stay in concentration.
- I am firmly rooted in life and I grow with each task. I show the world who I am.
- I am loving and caring with myself, my body, and my emotions.
- I take responsibility for my feelings as well as for my body.

The Sacral Chakra (7 – 14 yrs.)

Color: Orange
Endocrine Gland: Sex glands (testes, ovaries)
Function: Male/female distinctions, reproduction
Issues: Emotions and sexuality

The second lowest chakra is the Sacral. This vortex is strongly associated with and linked to one's sexuality and emotional self. The Sacral chakra deals with social and personal intimacy, sexuality, and reproduction. It matures between the ages of seven and fourteen. During this time, the child becomes aware of her differences. Likes, dislikes, and strong opinions are established.

A person with a healthy and balanced Sacral chakra will be joyful, friendly, and compassionate. They are emotionally satisfied and non-indulgent allowing them to be generous and giving. Balance in this chakra also manifests in creativity and playfulness.

An imbalance, either high or low, is often evident in a person who displays an extreme expression of emotions whether they be strong and brash or extremely reserved and quiet. Either extreme could be reflective of one whose Sacral chakra is out of balance. Any imbalances may lead to emotional or relationship problems, or sexual dysfunction.

Insufficient energy results in things like feelings of guilt, fear of change, being impulsive, or lacking excitement and passion. On the flip side, excessive energy may have you addicted to stimulation, having radical mood swings, or becoming emotionally dependent.

Affirmations you can use to help rebalance the Sacral chakra:

I will

repeat these

daily!

- I remain calm and collected, secure in the knowledge that everything comes in its own time.
- I know my body has its own inner wisdom, and that I am in good hands.
- I know my body will take good care of me.

- I know my strengths and weaknesses, and I accept them.

You might try thinking about one thing you could do that would create a sense of joy – then do it!

The Solar Plexus (14 – 21 yrs.)

Color: Yellow
Endocrine Gland: Adrenal
Function: Regulating stress
Issues: Power, energy

The third chakra is known as the Solar Plexus. According to Sanskrit teachings, it is associated with an energy body's self-esteem and self-confidence. Developing during the ages of fourteen to twenty-one, it includes the years of puberty and one's desires to break away from parents and become an individual. This chakra can help a person to feel his or her power.

A person with a healthy and balanced Solar Plexus will exude self-worth, self-esteem, and confidence. They will have courage and be able to make independent decisions, often relying on gut instinct. They can express their feelings without embarrassment.

An unhealthy, unbalanced Solar Plexus chakra may exhibit signs of insecurity, an excessive concern for what others think, and a constant need for reassurance. They may have a victim mentality and blame others for their misfortune if the energy is low. Or they may have situations of unprovoked temper tantrums or be prone to manipulating others if the energy is too high.

If you feel your Solar Plexus is out of balance, then every time you need to decide something consciously choose to check in with your energy. Place your hand over your solar plexus and ask, "Will this decision empower me or disempower me?" Affirmations for balancing the Solar Plexus include:

I will
repeat these
daily!

- I know I am a part of the whole. I feel and enjoy life with all my senses.
- I am better at saying what I mean. I do not get angry, but instead make constructive use of my displeasure.
- I am grateful for what I have and who I am.
- I do good for myself and pay attention to my needs.

The Heart Chakra (21 – 28 yrs.)
Color: Green
Endocrine Gland: Thymus
Function: Protection against autoimmunity
Issues: Love, compassion, connecting mind and body

The middle chakra, the Heart chakra, is cradled in the chest between the three lower chakras and the three upper chakras. It is no surprise that the primary areas of a person's life affected by the energy of this chakra are love and relationships. The Heart chakra deals with the right to love, forgiveness, and compassion. Characteristics of the Heart chakra include an ability for unconditional love, being emotionally balanced, and energized. Individuals with a balanced Heart chakra are patient, seek the truth, and have high integrity.

The Heart chakra is developed during the ages of twenty-one to twenty-eight. Commitment becomes important at this time, either to a career, a person, or both. Marriage and starting a family may occur.

Imagine a person who has a perfectly balanced Heart chakra. They are going to have unconditional love. Unconditional love doesn't necessarily mean that you have to love everyone and smother them with love. It just means that there is acceptance. You love them unconditionally, whatever their issues. It means compassion and being emotionally balanced. It means being content. You can have ups and downs but they are not huge peaks and huge valleys. Nothing knocks you off center. You are at peace. You are patient, truth-seeking, trusting, and in integrity with yourself. You are in your truth.

If you had an insufficiency or lack in the Heart Center there would be an imbalance. You may be overly reactive, lonely, or anti-social. You could be cold, distant, self-centered, and you would feel sorry for yourself, feel rejected, and have a lack of empathy. Some people call that heartless, cold-hearted, or having no feelings. A heart of stone. Greed is a symptom of a lack in the Heart Center too.

If you had an excess in the Heart chakra you could have mood swings, be demanding, overly critical, clingy, be over-sacrificing, or very intense. You want to give everything. This is also an imbalance and really not a happy state.

When you get a broken heart, that is an imbalance in the Heart chakra. Heartbreak can be either insufficient or excess depending on the person. If you are clinging and demanding and having mood swings what does that represent? What are you lacking or what do you have too much of? It can go either way here. This energy center is not the same as the other ones.

To rebalance the Heart chakra, you can practice random acts of kindness. They can be as simple as a smile to a stranger, giving a hug, or being sensitive to someone in need. These acts don't only need to be for others, you may also give yourself a gift of kindness like a compliment for something you've accomplished.

Heart chakra affirmations include:

I will

repeat these

daily!

- I am confident strength comes with each new task.
- I view obstacles and difficulties as incentives for inner growth and keep my eyes and ears open for new avenues.
- I make my way through fears, worries, anxieties, and grief. I know these feelings are a part of life, but I will not be stopped by them.
- I listen to my heart and the voice of love, light, and clarity.

The Throat Chakra (28 – 35 yrs.)

Color: Blue

Endocrine Gland: Thyroid

Function: Regulates metabolism and blood calcium levels

Issues: Communication, self-expression

According to Sanskrit teachings, the Throat chakra is all about self-expression and communication. It has to do with our ability to speak our truth, with being heard, and with listening. All forms of communication are expressed with the Throat chakra. It is located in the throat, above the heart. Some say the blue of this chakra is the breath of Jesus helping them to breathe in peace. This allows them to listen better, speak, and express their thoughts and ideas. The Throat chakra deals with the right to speak, to communicate, and the ability to trust. In the positive sense it has to do with the right to speak and to hear truth. In the negative sense it has to do with being lied to and lying. Some people tend to have a great deal of depression associated with this center.

Recall the Throat chakra develops between the ages of twenty-eight and thirty-five when creativity is strong and maturation takes place. There is an awareness that life is a manifestation of past choices.

A person with a balanced Throat chakra will display optimum communication skills and techniques. They are unafraid to communicate their needs or to express their opinions. Some of the characteristics are the ability to hear and express truth, creativity, willpower, and mental relaxation.

A blocked or imbalanced Throat chakra would hinder self-expression and communication including the ability to listen to others. It may cause a person to interpret or express information in an overly critical way and/or suppress their ability to communicate by becoming overly self-disciplined with what and how they share. Issues with imbalance could lead to not being able to voice or defend an opinion, not being heard, and overall trouble with communication of personal needs.

Low energy in the Throat chakra may manifest as a fear of speaking, being mistrustful of your intuitive powers, or not living in the present. High energy on the other hand may manifest in excessive talking, an inability to listen, being opinionated or self-righteous.

Affirmations related to the Throat chakra include:

I will

repeat these

daily!

- I feel lively even in hard times.
- I feel I am alive even in rough times and I keep moving on.
- I give my inner voice room to express itself.
- I listen to my inner voice.
- I am comfortable standing in and stating my truth.

The Third Eye Chakra (35 – 42 yrs.)
Color: Indigo
Endocrine Gland: Pineal Gland
Function: Produce melatonin, affect sleep/wake cycles

Issues: Intuition

The Third Eye chakra, also known as the Brow chakra, is located at the center of the forehead. This chakra is about intuition and inner wisdom. Its job is to perceive and interpret both the thoughts within oneself, and the world outside. Your Third Eye has to do with illusion. It has to do with your right to see. See what you want. Believe what you want. Developing between the ages of thirty-five and forty-two, it is the time for becoming an expert and for fine-tuning life.

This is our inner eye, the window to our soul. It deals with insights, developing psychic abilities, and releasing hidden and repressed negative thoughts. The expression *thoughts become things* is very appropriate to this center. If your thoughts had legs and were going to run out and get you everything you think about, what would you think about? This is our Third Eye – our manifestation. Good thoughts and bad thoughts.

This is also the place where we pick up energy or thoughts from other people, i.e. therapists from their clients or a wife from her husband. A parent can have intuition with their child. This center can take anything in, but you must consciously decipher what you want. The Third Eye will always try to prove everything right. It wants to make every thought, feeling, or belief become true. It is your subconscious mind wishing to please you. This is why you must be vigilant and choose what thoughts you really desire to manifest.

A person who is highly intuitive or can see clearly the world that surrounds them most likely has a healthy and balanced Third Eye chakra. An unhealthy Third Eye chakra is often evident in a person who is too logical, arrogant, undisciplined, or refuses to see the big picture. Imbalances may cause disconnection with Spirit, blocked intuition, and closed-off psychic abilities.

Affirmations for balancing the Third Eye chakra include:

I will

repeat these

daily!

- I gladly reach out to others to complement and enrich my personal development.
- I know my strength and use it wisely to keep my body and soul in harmony.
- I relax and let things go, this gives me new strength.
- I take care of my body and respect its signals. They show my soul the right way.
- I remain calm, balanced, and centered because I know my strength performs best from my center.

The Crown Chakra (42 – 49 yrs.)

Color: Violet or White

Endocrine Gland: Pituitary

Function: Controls growth, blood pressure, pregnancy, breast milk production, sex organs, thyroid gland, conversion of food to energy, water regulation, absorption of water into the kidneys, body temperature

Issues: Wisdom, bliss, awareness, consciousness, spiritual connection

The Crown chakra, also known as the 7th chakra, is located at the top of the head. This chakra strengthens the spirituality and selflessness within an individual. Opening and keeping this chakra balanced is not a destination, it simply allows for more enlightenment in oneself. The Crown chakra is all about connecting with higher consciousness, with becoming connected to the higher-self and connecting to the etheric body.

This energy center is our connection between spiritual planes. If you've ever been daydreaming or lost in your head, you are in the Crown chakra. Here you are working with the subconscious. This center is active when you are dreaming or in hypnosis.

The Crown chakra is being developed between the ages of forty-two and forty-nine. The end of the first seven life cycles at the age of forty-nine signifies the middle of life. It is during this time that the "mid-life" crisis generally occurs. This seven-year chakra cycle repeats after age forty-nine, although in this phase it focuses primarily on spiritual development and fulfillment before death.

A person with a balanced Crown chakra is open to life and spirituality. They have an awareness of both themselves and the world. Their emotions are stabilized and they have peace and spiritual insight. They are in touch with their higher-mind and have attained a state of personal power.

An individual with a blocked Crown chakra does not experience her spirituality and thus loses her sense of "belonging." She may have chronic anxiety, indecisiveness, and a lack of joy. Low energy in this chakra shows characteristics of boredom, uncertainty and lack of purpose, being depressed, or a fear of death. An imbalance on the high side may result in being irritable, overly intellectual, disassociation from the body, or having a spiritual addiction.

In addition to the affirmations that follow, you might try meditating in silence, using Oracle cards to connect with your higher-self, listen to guided visualizations, or color a mandala to bring this chakra back into balance.

- I trust that I am well-guided to my goals.
- I am grateful for the material goods in my life, and I use them intelligently as resources on my journey through life.
- I see reality with open eyes. I stay alert and focus on my aims.
- I orient my thoughts and actions to a higher wisdom and place my ego at its service.

Mandala Exercise

Sometimes I get stuck or confused about a question or something I need to decide. I can't seem to come up with an answer. I'm too much in my head with too many ifs, buts, and whys. I can't seem to get into the truth or my higher-self. I can't seem to get unblocked from coming up with the right answer because my ego keeps trying to get involved. When this happens, I often use the mandala exercise. See if it will work for you.

Take a black and white mandala, one that you need to color. The more detailed the better. You can use less detailed ones, but I find sometimes it takes a bit longer for me to get out of my head and into my heart, so more detail allows me the time to get to my truth. On the back of the mandala, write your problem or concern for which you want an answer. Then give it up to Spirit or your higher-self. Turn the mandala over and begin to color. Don't think about the question. Don't think about the answer. Think only about the mandala – the shapes, patterns, colors. This will take you out of your left brain and into your right brain. It's amazing how by the time I'm finished with the mandala, out of nowhere the answers come or the solutions appear. For me, 95% of the time it's always what I need to hear or know.

I've included one of my favorite mandalas on the opposite page for you to try.

The Way Chakras Work

Remember that we are spiritual beings having a human experience. We are indeed living in a dual reality. These energy centers are meant to be in flux, like a pendulum. They are flowing. We all desire to be in perfect balance and harmony. We all say we want that. But truly, do you want to go through life and never be so overjoyed, so happy, or laughing hysterically with a friend? Of course not. Do you never want to feel pain or loss? Of course not. Without these extremes both ways we would not have a clue what "normal" is.

59 Chakras

As a spiritual being having a human experience, these energy centers keep us in our bodies and active yet allow us to go between realities. They help us create our existence. Yes, we are going to have a desire to be in our lighter, happier self. We are going to have desires to be connected to that lighter energy. We are also going to desire to avoid pain. But being here means we are here to experience these lessons. We are here to touch the lives with whom we share these experiences. We are here to be part of these situations.

Whether you rear-end somebody or they rear-end you, it's not a happy moment but it is a physical and human experience. What lessons and understandings are you here to learn from it? These situations are meant to remind us of our truth. They are just experiences.

What happens if you're going through life and you get happy and your pendulum swings over to one side – the excess energy side? Then the excitement is over and you start coming down and back to neutral. You are content, balanced, and feeling good. Then you're going about your day and BOOM you have a tire blow out on the freeway. This throws the pendulum over to the other side – the low energy side. You do not feel very happy at this point. Maybe you feel angry or scared and you don't know what to do. You don't know if anyone will help you. There is fear and anxiety or maybe sadness and helplessness.

Whatever the emotion is, it is not in the Light. It is not making the world a better place. Being in that dark space is ugly and it is that way not only for you, but most likely for anyone around you including the person you called for help. In a situation when you are scared and angry you are not going to be calling someone in a carefree or blithe manner. Instead you will have an intensity about you. That's okay, it just means you are more in your ego. You're having a human experience. End of story. We are designed to have these experiences.

But, we are also designed to go back to the center relatively quickly. Our energy fields are built to recover from anything emotional that happens to us. They are designed to recover us within a ten percent margin.

If you experienced the death of someone close to you, then you are going to get thrown over to the negative side. It's going to take more time to recover and get back to center as you need a grieving period. Getting back to center, or neutral, would take less time if you heard someone you hardly knew had died. You would most likely be able to return relatively soon. But when it is somebody you're wholly attached to, and don't even want to think about being without, you're going to grieve. You're going to be stuck there for a while until you can remember the good times, until you can remember the happy times. That is why it is important when we are in a negative state of loss to remember to celebrate life, surround ourselves with things that bring us up and move ourselves to a more positive mode as soon as possible. The vibration of laughter helps pull us out of the dark and recover to neutral faster.

Whether we are high or low, we are always trying to use the pull of the pendulum to return to a neutral state of energy. You may not get all of the way back over to the positive side, but you would at least not be as sad. Something I try to remember is pain is inevitable, suffering is optional. We can help ourselves move out of situations by remembering the truth, the light, happy times, and good memories. This is our job knowing that we are spiritual beings having a human experience. When you get caught up in the moment of the physical experience remember it is your job to acknowledge that you are having a human moment. Know that you are in your ego/physical side and that's okay.

During these not so pleasant human experiences, you don't need to wait for someone to point out how terrible or heavy your attitude is. I find it best to learn to recognize and own your feelings.

Reality Check Exercise

Ask yourself to wait a minute; to just hold on a second. Then ask yourself, "How do I feel? Is this mine? Is this my truth? Do I have a reason to feel this way?" and if your answer is 'yes' then the question is "Why am I feeling this way?" Then the big question "What would it take to get me over to the positive side or to let this go?" What would it take? Who can do that for you? Nobody else, just you. Too often we wait for people to do this for us. We wait for them to make suggestions or read our minds. Waiting for others to do it for us is not our truth. It is just our ego trying to manipulate to get our needs met.

Taking personal responsibility is not cutting everyone else off. It is healthy and positive. It can, however, be good to ask for what we need. Asking is different from expecting others to provide our needs automatically. You can say to a good friend, "Hey, Susie, I really need you to compliment me today. I just don't know why. My ego says I'm feeling down and I need somebody to make me feel good." Is there anything wrong with that? No, because you are trying to meet your need. It does not matter why you are feeling the way you are. Remember, it is a human experience. As soon as you're done with it you move back in to your dual reality. There is no judgment of the experience. We acknowledge it and move on.

There is nothing wrong with seeking outside of ourselves to have our needs met if doing so is done with the right intention. You can say to someone, "I'm just having a bad day and I need this or that" or "I need you to do this for me." At that point they have the right to refuse it, or even to not participate.

That might swing you further out to the negative side, but it could be exactly what you needed to take your power back.

Let's say they do throw you back into the negative or deeper into anger or despair. You can revisit the situation or experience and ask again, "What would it take? What do I need to get me back to the positive side?" Maybe you need to go through old photos of when you were in the positive and ask yourself, "How can I feel like that again?" Maybe you need to do a quick meditation. Maybe you need to talk to someone else. Maybe you need to exercise. There are dozens of other ideas and techniques you could use to shift the pendulum.

More importantly, ask yourself, "Am I willing to do what it takes to get there?" If the answer is no for any reason, then it may not be that important to you to shift or the timing is off. It is what it is. Accept it and just go on about your day. You have now taken your pendulum and moved your energy centers because you have made a choice.

Sometimes multiple good experiences happen in a series. Then suddenly something bad happens. You could have three good memories and two bad, then five good memories and two bad. Just keep coming back to center. It will be more likely you will be a positive person and in a positive space than a negative person if you do. There is no judgment. Whatever your life experiences are and how you feel about them, is what is creating the environment you will be in.

If you are like the dragonfly and you have emerged from an extended period in the dark waters, or a lot of negative experiences, or a negative energy environment, then your vibration is going to be different than those who are still in that dark place. It does not make those people bad or wrong. It just means they are where they are. You are at a different level, a different mode of experience.

But we also know that if they have all this bad stuff, they also have the ability all the while to focus on their spirit side and their truth. If they continue to remain stuck, their focus is elsewhere. Their beliefs are elsewhere. They are not broken. They are not bad nor good. They are in their place and not where you are. Maybe they choose to live there. It's a choice. One choice is going to make you happy and one is going to make you not so happy.

In could be those people only think they are happy because they do not remember their positive and happy place. They have forgotten the positive side of the pendulum and their spiritual side. They don't remember they have the power to move the pendulum in the direction they choose. I hope that everyone reading this book will remember. I hope you remember that just because you are a product of your past and you are a product of your environment, it has absolutely nothing to do with who you choose to be from this moment forward.

You can choose to live in your traumas, your history, your beliefs, or you can choose to live in the other side, your true side and reflect those beautiful colors for the world to see. You can accept the good with the bad and yet choose to focus on the positive. What you focus on you will get more of. Even with every awful situation, there is something good. You can make any situation what you want. This is because your thoughts do have legs and everything you think about you are bringing about, good, bad, or indifferent. Remember, the subconscious mind always proves you right. If you say "I'm always wrong" you're right. If you say "I'm hot" you're right. If you say, "I am a wise, beautiful, powerful being" you are right (and you are!).

Think about your energy centers, your chakras. Where do you have your weakness? Where do you feel out of balance? Then try this exercise. Write a letter to yourself using the following salutation:

> *Oh, wise, beautiful, and powerful King/Queen [your name],*

Then begin your letter. Write in the letter exactly what you want from each chakra that you feel is not in balance, whether that energy is too low or too high. Do not place any limitations on yourself. Write your desires regardless if they seem reasonable or attainable. These are your desires, there is no right or wrong.

Once your letter is complete, take a moment to

ponder what will happen if nothing in your letter comes to fruition. What's your life going to be like? How will you feel if none of this happens? You might want to write this down as well.

Then take a moment to think about what if it *does* happen? What will your life look like then? If you do get what you want, how will you feel? With a simple yes or no, with every beat of your heart, are you willing to allow it?

Check in with yourself that you're answering yes or no without putting conditions on your answer. No yes, I'll allow it if this or I'll allow it if that. Regardless of how it shows up, I'm going to stand in the light of my desires and I'm going to focus on obtaining them.

If you added conditions or found upon reflection that nothing would really change in your life, then either your chakra is not significantly out of balance or you are not being completely in your truth in defining your desires. If, however, you know a significant change would be of benefit and you are committed to allowing it to happen, then it is time to engage your Soul chakra.

The Soul Chakra

The Soul chakra, also known as the eighth chakra, is located about an arms-length above your head. It is considered the seat of the soul; the point where spiritual energy and Divine love enter the body.

This is the chakra you are going to be connecting with in order to shift old beliefs and patterns and attain your desires.

The Soul chakra communicates with us through images, patterns, numbers, symbols, and archetypes. The Dragonfly is a symbol for me. When I ask a question of the Soul chakra, the dragonfly inevitably shows up somewhere, although not always. Regardless of the symbol, it shows up in threes for me.

This morning, of all things, it was the monkey. At breakfast, my daughters and I were laughing about a story about a monkey. I look up at the TV and I'm like, "Is that a cat? Oh my gosh, it's a monkey. What's a monkey doing on TV?" I walk in to my room and there's a pamphlet from Animal Planet, all about the monkey. It's probably been there for a day or two and I haven't paid any attention to it. I realize this is not a coincidence. I go and look up the monkey in my book of animal totems to understand the message.

Seeing the monkey was a synchronistic event reminding me of my connection to God, Spirit, Source. You can ask for any symbol you want to know you're connected to Spirit, the angels, your Source. It might be pennies, dimes, butterflies, or dragonflies. When you do this, you're connected to the higher Soul chakra. This chakra contains the seeds of our soul's purpose and life purpose. By healing and clearing the Soul chakra which carries information, one life into another, we make sure that we do not repeat the same lessons again and again. Through this chakra we can uncover and heal soul damage. By working with the Soul chakra, we can have access to our soul's destiny. We can receive inspiration and greater insights into our life. We can also work hand-in-hand with our soul to create the life of our dreams.

Now that you have your letter of all your desires, let's do a little meditation to connect to your Soul chakra. You will be clearing out all negative vibrations and energies of your past including all cellular memories and imprints. You will let them go. You will go into the meditation with the intension of creating what you want and being clear. You will only take what is true for you and what is aligned with your intension.

Clearing the Soul Chakra

Close your eyes and place your attention on your Soul chakra located approximately 1 arm's length above the head. Breathe into it. Allow yourself to connect to your Soul chakra. Take a moment to just notice what this white chakra feels or maybe looks like. Now allow yourself to become aware of what blocks or information it holds. Allow any necessary insights or communications to flood into your mind. Repeat with me, _divine wisdom, I ask you to go really deep into my soul chakra and expose any damage_ *to my soul, trauma, density, and negative programs I may be carrying. If there are any blocks to me experiencing my life's purpose fully, grandly, and passionately, please remove them.*

As you continue to tune into this chakra, allow yourself to become aware of any cracks in it. Imagine that you are given a bottle of healing gold liquid. Pour the liquid into the chakra, allow it to repair and clear away any damage. Observe it happening. When the damage has been cleared, notice the magnificence of your soul. Become aware of the purity, holiness, and love your soul embodies. Allow yourself to touch your soul, hold it, and dance with it. As you dance with it, allow it to clear the way for you to discover your soul's purpose and your soul's wisdom.

Now focus on your breath. The deeper and more connected to your breath, the more you awaken your body's divine wisdom allowing it to merge with your soul. Take it all in, feel it move through every cell of your body. Welcome it. Now repeat with me, *I now connect to my divine wisdom which guides me to the most healing, loving, and expansive experiences. I am ready to welcome wellbeing into my life on all levels. I now attract people and events into my life that help me to achieve my soul purpose. Thank you, Divine Spirit.*

When you are ready either allow yourself to gently come back, knowing that you have connected to your body and soul on all levels. You have worked on healing, clearing, and rejuvenating your chakras which allows you to expand your life's journey and attract wonderful experiences and empowering people into your life. Remember it takes time and patience to release dense energy so persevere with your healing and enjoy the process of self-discovery.

The Power of Color

Like all things, colors are energy and vibrate to their own frequency. That is why they have different effects psychologically. Lighting candles of different colors has been used in religious and ceremonial rituals for this reason. Colors solicit responses in our psyche, our mind, and our spirit.

At the same time, each of us is vibrating at a different frequency. This is why we perceive colors and are affected by them differently. Colors can also have general meanings, associations, and psychological effects because we all share many of the same psychological structures. We live on the same planet, under the same sky and sun. We have, more or less, the same internal organs. We feel the same emotions and instincts, just in different ways. There are basic levels of life that we all experience – both as good things and as bad ones.

Studies have been done in universities around the world that show dramatic behavioral differences occur when an individual is exposed to different colors. Some of the general results of these tests were:

- Red invoked anxiety and impatience. Red also generated a lot of energy. This could be why waiting at a red traffic light seems to take so long.
- Orange was soothing and healing. People felt it was a "festive" color.
- Yellow was found to be intellectually stimulating.
- Green was refreshing and generated a feeling of vitality.
- Blue was peaceful and they found a baby in a blue room would sleep through the night without interruption.
- Purple gave a sense of confidence and self-esteem.
- Pink would calm a violent person when put in a pink room for a short time.
- Black caused fear and suppression.
- Brown was "earthy," stable, and consistent.
- White was found to create purity and made people feel fresh and renewed.

In addition to these findings, there are many other associations in general, as well as ones I have collected through my observations such as:

- Red – the right to be here and own your own space.
- Orange – guilt, the right to feel.

- Yellow – the right to act and stand in your power and act on your desires and wishes, shame.
- Green – The right to love and be loved, sorrow.
- Blue – calming, soothing, cool.
- Indigo – mysterious, unknown.
- Purple – introspective.
- White – purity, peace, Spirit, attachment.

As we learned in the last chapter, each of the primary chakras is associated with a specific color. This color frequency is aligned with the neutral frequency of the chakra it represents – in essence the color represents a chakra that is in balance. The actual colors fall into two distinct classical elements that are polar opposites – fire and water.

If you were paying attention, you would notice that the colors red, orange, and yellow correspond to the lower chakras – the Root, Sacral, and Solar Plexus. These are the colors of fire. Fire rises toward the Heart. Above the Heart chakra are the colors blue, indigo, and violet or white. These are the colors of water representing the Throat, Third Eye, and Crown chakras. Water runs down toward the Heart.

In the center is the Heart, the color green, forming a bridge between the Fire and Water. Blue from the Throat chakra blending with yellow from the Solar Plexus makes green. Even though it sits where your heart would be, it is the center of the chakra energy.

It is not your heart, yet it is connected to your heart. This is all about a sense of unity, community, compassion, being loved, and being loving. Your dreams and desires are a part of this center.

Another energy center sits right behind the green Heart chakra. This is like a second heart chakra and vibrates to the color pink. This energy center is all about unconditional love of self and others.

Color is a powerful tool in bringing your chakras, your energy centers back into balance. When you have low energy in your lower chakras, something is insufficient. You can boost that energy by adding more of the same color to make it bolder. On the other hand, if you have an excessive amount of energy, you'll want to tone it back down by using the opposite color. Water puts out fire, and fire heats up water.

For example, let's say the color yellow in your Solar Plexus is vibrating at a low frequency. It will be dim and lacking in vibrancy. To bring it back into balance we might want to wear a bright yellow scarf, or we may want to stand in the bright yellow light of the sun. If we have an excess of this fire energy the color will already be brilliantly bright. We'd want to bring it back to center by using a water color. Perhaps we'd put on an indigo blue or purple scarf, or we might stand by a lake, or look up to the sky on a cloudless night. The same would be true in your upper chakras. If you are feeling sad or melancholic, you would not want to add more blue, you would want to add yellow to cheer you up.

Dragonfly and Color

The bright colors of a dragonfly take time to develop. It is not until they have chosen to emerge from the dark that their colors become visible. The same is true for us. Only with personal growth and maturity will our true colors shine forth.

Dragonflies love the light. They are only out during the day and most of their activity is during the summer. This animal spirit teaches us special ways we can use the light, reflect it, and even shape it. They represent the ability to reform the light around us; to reshape the light of our environment into something new and beautiful.

Structures in the dragonfly's skin refract light the same way moisture in the air makes a rainbow. It is as if there are tiny prisms in its skin. Their ability to both reflect and refract light and colors have caused the dragonfly to be associated with many forms of magic and mysticism. Dragonflies teach us that we are Light beings and can reflect the outside light as well as our inner light in wonderful ways.

The dragonfly also teaches us how to connect with the powers of color and how to work with different colors to achieve our desires. Here we learn how the colors we wear, the colors we fill our homes with, and the colors of the cars we drive all impact us. Dragonfly people will benefit from working with colors and crystals. Crystals refract light in similar ways as the dragonfly. In one sense, crystals are solidified colors.

If someone's aura, the glow of energy that surrounds them, seems depleted of color and vital energy, a person with a dragonfly totem can help them to draw in all of the colors, both physical colors and spiritual colors. This can repair and strengthen the aura.

Color is one thing that feeds the aura. Color helps the aura become stronger and healthier. Working with colors on a regular basis can be very healing and uplifting.

Emotions are often described as colors. For example, we say we "feel blue" or are "tickled pink." Dragonfly people tend to be very gifted at helping others navigate their emotional waters. A dragonfly has the ability to take in a color and reflect out its essential beauty.

By looking at what colors a person surrounds themselves with it is easy to reveal what emotions are dominant in their life. What colors do you wear? What colors do you decorate your home in? What colors are in your workplace? What colors do you think about?

Many emotional states can remain in a person's psyche for a long time. Sometimes, we forget about them but continue to carry them without knowing where they originated. They could have been caused by events from long ago. This can cause us to project these emotions onto others and to attract people with the same emotions into our lives. Dragonfly energy helps us uncover these old emotions.

Emotions also influence the colors of the aura. A dragonfly person can help someone to release energy that is harmful and teach someone to gain energies that will be of service. The key with dragonfly energy and color is that dragonfly energy is about showing your true colors. This is how we emerge into and become our true selves.

The dragonfly's power of emergence means that what is emerging within you is the sense of your inner strength and true nature. This is the spiritual part of you. As it comes out it expands and helps you to know and understand who you really are. It is a beautiful and powerful journey as we live and express it.

Working with Color

Before we can work effectively with color to put our chakras, our energies, back into balance, we need to understand how different colors make us feel. If possible, I'd like you to do a little experiment with color before we move on.

Color Exercise

With your eyes closed, place a solid colored scarf, cloth, or garment over your eyes. Tilt your head back, look up toward a light and open your eyes. Take in a few deep breaths, then sit quietly and take as much time as you need to allow yourself to notice how this color makes you feel mentally, emotionally, physically, and spiritually. Allow yourself to come back to full waking consciousness. Write down these feelings. If the feelings are anything other than positive, write down below them how you would rather feel if it is different. Continue to do this exercise with several other colors. Remember to breathe through each one, take your time, and let your true knowing invoke your feelings. There is no right or wrong answer. It is perfectly okay to own your truth and feel how you feel.

Did one color make you feel energized? Depressed? Scared? Smothered? Playful? Confused? Hot? Did a color bring up memories? The key is to have an awareness of how the color makes you feel. Sometimes we do not like a color because its energy is something in which we are deficient. We can be opposed to the very thing we need. For instance, purple may feel heavy and weighted. You do not like it, yet you suffer from anxiety. Anxiety is an orange/yellow energy. You may feel okay in those colors, but would you want to add more fire to your being during an anxiety attack? Or would a little grounding be better to pull you back to a calmer state?

We may indeed need to use the colors we don't like to bring ourselves into balance. We need to experience them, pay attention to them, and really connect. Once we feel the association of the truth of the color and the energy, we can change our perspective and relation to that color. We can lose any negative associations with it.

Keep in mind that colors have different meanings for each of us. This is why we can't make a perfect environment for anyone else. We only need to make a perfect environment for ourselves. By studying colors though, we might be able to come close to perfection for others too. It is important to remember also, that the meanings of colors change as our energy and vibrational frequencies change. What appeals to you today may no longer appeal the further along you are on your journey to the Light.

Think about what your favorite color was at different phases in your life. What was it when you were a young child, versus a teenager, versus what it is now? Your favorite color has probably changed a multitude of times. It can even come back to what it was before for entirely different reasons. Changes of color preference make a huge difference and can be guideposts to where your energies are in or out of balance.

Continually wearing dull, drab colors while asking for more adventures or excitement in life sends the message that we do not really want what we are asking for. The colors we surround ourselves with set up a vibration that attracts circumstances and energies that reflect to us the messages we are transmitting. If we want to change, we need to affirm that we are ready and willing for the changes to occur. We can do this through the use of colors whose vibrations match the energy we are seeking to experience.

If you want to become known for the work you love doing then wearing shades of red or violet will help. For new beginnings, try wearing shades of green. Shades of yellow are effective to feel more empowered. For a deeper connection to the Universe and to develop greater intuitive ability, all shades of blues and indigo are excellent!

Color is a valuable tool in expressing who we are, who we desire to be, and what we desire to experience. All of nature sets forth its intent and requests through the use of a vast range of color. A flower will attract a pollinator, a frog may warn predators that it is not good to eat, and a lion can attract a mate all through color. The dragonfly can teach us how to use color to attract what we desire or to understand at least what messages we are sending into the universe by the colors we wear and surround ourselves with.

Color Conscious Choosing

Choosing which colors to wear, carry, or surround yourself with takes more than the knowledge of how the color makes you feel. You must go back to elementary school and remember the color wheel. If you recall, balancing your energy requires either intensifying the color of the energy if you are lacking, or toning down the energy of the color if you have excess. You would need to use the opposite color from the color wheel because this is the color that would balance you. These colors are also called complementary colors.

For example, red and green are opposites. These are the Christmas colors. Red as the Root chakra color means security and safety. Green is the whole heart meaning love and togetherness. For many, Christmas represents a time of happiness, unity, joy, and family.

Orange and blue are opposites. Blue helps with communicating. Orange helps us to be expressive and emotionally satisfied.

Yellow and purple are the next pair of opposites. These are the colors of the Solar Plexus and Crown (violet, a variation of purple) or Third Eye chakras. These are the top points of our physical and spiritual selves.

The Heart Center is like a seesaw. It's the balancing point. It goes between the Root and the Crown. When you take the three major points, the Root,

Heart, and Crown, the colors are red, green, and purple. This color combination makes magenta. Magenta is the bridge color. It is the oscillation between infrared and ultraviolet. Magenta shares the same root word with magnetic and magic. It is used for inner transformation and making changes. It is an excellent color for connection.

If it helps, you might also look at the color wheel as an overlay of the Sun's cycle and the way the Sun changes colors throughout the day. When the Sun rises the colors in the sky are sunny. They are bright reds and oranges. In the middle of the day the Sun moves through the greens, until at sunset you get into the range of purples. People who resonate with brighter colors will be morning people, while people who resonate with darker colors will function better at night. What colors give you energy? Does this match with the time of day that you function best?

These colors that we're playing with are important when we are trying to create balance in our lives. If you had an imbalance in the Throat chakra, which vibrates to the color blue, the imbalance could be because you are having an insufficiency or an excess. Take note of the affirmations that resonate with you for clues. If the Throat chakra is just not as vibrant as you want it to be, you could add blue to make it stronger. This acts homeopathically to help bring you out of that imbalance and into balance.

For an insufficiency, such as the symptoms of depression and feeling blue, you would not want to add more of the color blue to your life as there is already too much water. Water equals emotions and no one wants to be waterlogged with negative emotions. When most are sad, they would rather be glad. So, orange is your new best friend, even if it's uncomfortable and you can only handle it in small doses. Don't give up!

Orange brings joy and happiness. When we say we feel blue it means we feel down so joy and happiness bring us back up. Orange works in both ways. The polar opposite color can be used to empower. It is the other pull of the pendulum.

If you had an excess of energy in your Throat chakra, it could mean you are very strong in your voice and that could be overpowering. You may even feel the need to shout out injustice. In this instance, you would add blue to calm down the misplaced fire energy.

People with a great deal of purple tend to be too much in thought, too much in their head, and lacking joy. Adding some yellow helps balance that by allowing them to express their feelings. People who are workaholics and unattached spend a lot of time in their head. Yellow is a great color to bring in because it is going to bring out their true desires and wants on an emotional level.

Being in your head isn't always a bad thing. People

like writers need to be in their head to create the stories they write. Sometimes, however, that may result in a block, writer's block. Bringing in yellow at that point will help to unlock the block so that the words will flow freely again.

One example of using colors to enhance yourself or give you a certain type of energy is the Power Tie. A power tie usually is strong in the color red. Remember that red is about energy, passion, strength, and of course power. When you put on your power tie you feel like you are ten feet tall. You walk in like you own the place. And you feel powerful enough to own the room.

You look just like the big corporate boss, who also has a red tie. People know he's the one in charge. People respect him. They do not worship him because of his tie, but he sure thinks so. And that's good. He is using the color with intention. If someone wanted to be the big boss, they would follow him, and watch every move he makes.

But be careful. You may think the guy in the red tie is powerful but what if you were victimized by someone in red, such as a red shirt? Then you are likely to fear that person. You may even hate the red-tie boss. You may not like the color red and not remember why you don't like it.

If you wear a particular color, there is a fifty-fifty chance of the person with whom you are interacting to respond to the energy the way you want.

Luckily, there are many other factors, such as body language, voice, emotional energy, your mental state, and the environment you are in which add more probability to your desired outcome. They will have a positive or negative reaction or be neutral.

They could have just come from a trauma unit and seen blood all day. But what if they just got some Valentines? The color red would have very different meanings. Regardless of the impact of your color choices on other people, it is always more important to focus on what the colors mean to you personally. Therein lies your personal power!

Conscious color choosing is intentionally using colors for a purpose. This action is something you can do in the morning when you wake up and you want to plan and create your day with intentions. (I'll talk more about intentions later.) You pick out the colors you are going to wear and the colors you will have with you. You pick the colors you will be around. All of these colors can be selected to build the type of day you will have based on the energies and feelings of the colors.

In the morning ask yourself, "How do I want to feel today? What do I need?" If you are tired then what color would energize you? What if you are taking a class and you need to study or concentrate? What color would you use? What if you wanted to feel relaxed because you were going into a stressful environment? What color would you use if you wanted to create some art?

Maybe today you wear orange to feel energized. Tomorrow you might wear blue to feel the same way. You might wear pink underwear just because you felt you needed pink. All the colors have different associations. Depending on your needs several colors or combinations might be in order. Perhaps you need some tie-dye so you can feel all the colors.

If there is an aggression imbalance, such as too much anger or greed then there is too much fire. Some people will say "You need to cool off." When there is too much of this type of energy you can tone it down with green, because green is the opposite of red which is fire. Green is neutral, the color of peace and harmony.

Let's try another exercise to see how color might help.

Color Exercise

Think about an early childhood moment. Visualize the home you grew up in, the people who were around you, and what you were like as a child. Look at your positive characteristics, the ones you possessed then, versus the ones you have now. Write them all down. Think about who you were and who you have become. Take note of how the answers make you feel. Now, think about times you had a fear of change or you lacked energy. What was going on?

The key is to look at the insufficiencies versus the excesses. You do not need to have characteristics of insufficiency or excess in all categories. For example, in the Root, on the excess side you could be overeating, have a lack of energy, fear any change, and be addicted to security, but not be aggressive or greedy. You could look at what color it would take to be energized versus lacking energy. What color would it take for you not to be afraid and to change? What color is it like to feel secure? Are you willing to do the work and make the change?

You want to get yourself to neutral. You don't want to be lacking energy and replacing it with another negative pattern or throwing yourself into the other extreme of insufficiency, like being ungrounded. Adding more of the color red to your life at this point wouldn't make sense. You could add green to bring yourself closer to normal.

Often, when we have so many imbalances on the excess side, we'll tend to throw ourselves into the insufficiencies side because we're trying to self-correct. We may use so much of a certain color or colors that the pendulum swings too far. That's when we find ourselves on a roller coaster of emotion.

When you look at the imbalances do not focus on why they happened. You do not need to tell or retell that story. What would it take to be okay with it? What would you need? If you had courage would you fear change? What would it take for you to feel courage? If you have determination would you overeat? If you were assertive would you be addicted to security? If you had good health would you lack energy? If you felt stable would you need to feel greedy?

Since color is such an important part of our lives and well-being, here is one more list of colors and their meanings to help you select the right ones when balancing your energy.

Aqua is for metaphysics, mind, magic, peace, reflection.

Black is for banishing.

Blue is for balance, healing, tranquility, soothing, electric, justice, astral projection, wisdom.

Brown is for grounding, home, and animals.

Copper is for passion, career, growth, business success.

Green is for beauty, fertility, prosperity, nature, money, balance, mental and emotional harmony, rejuvenation.

Indigo is for perception, inspiration, intuition, spirituality, psychic powers, idealism, understanding, reducing phobias.

Lavender is for knowledge, spiritual protection, intuition, calming.

Magenta is for inner transformation and making changes.

Orange is for creativity, attraction, legal matters, cheering, expansion, freeing, relieving repressions, creative thinking, optimism, harvesting.

Peach is for gentleness, joy, friendship, children.

Pink is for love, friendship, fidelity.

Purple is for psychic ability, spiritual growth and awareness, wisdom, independence, tolerance, regality, authority.

Red is for lust, courage, love, energy, vitality, willpower, strength, passion, creativity, action, leadership, transformation.

Rose is for self-love, relationships.

Silver is for psychic protection, removing negativity.

Violet is for spirit, etheric, esoteric, ancient wisdom, mysteries, power, wealth, meditation, reflections.

White is for purity, protection, truth, inner peace, meditation.

Yellow is for confidence, visions, mental powers, mind, knowledge, concentration, depression relief, pain relief, travel.

Wheel of Needs

What do we need? What do we want more of? What do we want less of? Our needs are held in the chakras below the Heart - Root, Sacral, and Solar Plexus. The chakras above the Heart hold our desires. When working with the energy of your needs, it helps to have clarity about where you are starting from, and where you are going to. We use a tool called the Wheel of Needs to do this.

Wheel of Needs

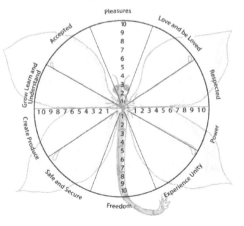

The wheel is a circle divided into ten pieces of pie if you will. At the top of the circle is Pleasure, then working clockwise comes Love and be Loved, Respect, Power, Experience Unity, Freedom, Safe and Secure, Create/Produce, Grow, Learn and Understand, and Accepted. Each slice of the pie is dissected by a line with the numbers 1 through 10, with 1 at the center of the circle and 10 at the circle's edge. Number 1 is the least fulfilled and number 10 is when you are so full there is no room for more.

For each of the categories you would select the number that most closely matches how you feel. Let's say you pick the number seven in the Pleasures category. Draw a line across the seven and color in the space below. Do the same for each of the other categories. Once you've colored everything in, it will be obvious which needs are not being fulfilled and where your wheel is out of balance.

When you do your Wheel of Needs, chances are you will find that there is room for improvement. You will probably see that there are areas in your life where all your needs are not 100% fulfilled. We all have some unmet needs to various degrees, and our needs change all the time. We are always moving up and down and all around on the Wheel. For this reason, it is helpful to check in on a regular basis with your Wheel.

Sometimes you could be high in one area and low in another. Other times you could move up on an area you were low in and not make any movement in another. We need to be constantly aware of where we are. In this way we are always strengthening our wheel. Wheels need to be round and firm so they can roll properly. You want a full, round wheel to ride on, not a flat tire.

If your Wheel looks a little floppy that's okay. Just acknowledge that there are some areas that could use a boost. There are always opportunities for improvement. Do not feel discouraged and do not say, "I need to work on this." The word "need" used this way does not imply that any action will be taken. I know it's called a Wheel of Needs. It represents what we need. Making changes to your Wheel requires commitment and action.

Instead of saying "I need to," you could say, "I am in process" or "I now choose to change this." The key to success is in owning it and deciding what is and is not acceptable. When we say we need to do something it means we accept it as it is. It doesn't mean we've committed to making a change or a shift.

Is anything in your Wheel bothering you enough for you to commit to making a change? When it does, that is when change happens. That is when improvement happens. Good, bad, or indifferent, once we commit to something, whether it's a bad relationship, bad job, or being healthy, or going on vacation, a decision has to be made to either stay the same, get worse, or get better. Are you willing to say, "I am going to" or "I am changing this" or "It's already done?" Look at your Wheel of Needs and examine which areas you can commit to changing. Then ask what it would take to raise it to a 10. Be willing, be ready!

However, if you are starting at a 2 then you probably won't be able to think about getting to 10 right away. That would be overwhelming. Just take it to the next level. Get to 3, and when you get there, then move to 4. You don't need to try to jump to 10. You just want to stretch your mind to formulate a strategy that will eventually get you to 10. You can do it in steps. You want to be able to imagine yourself at 10 and know you can get there. Know you will. Believe it and begin the steps, even if they are baby ones.

What does it take to get to 10? It takes commitment and it takes a decision. You have to decide that you are no longer going to settle for where you are. Decide that you are not going to allow anything to disempower you. Decide what you are going to do. It can be any direction or any decision. There is no right or wrong.

For example, you could decide that travel is not that important and you do not want to work for it. Therefore, you are completely fulfilled because you do not need it. That is great! You are where you want to be. But, if you are at a number that is not completely fulfilled, it is important to work on it if you want to keep growing and transitioning into your highest and best self. You are not going to be able to fly too well with those imbalanced wings. You are not going to have a life of ease. You are not going to have a life of joy. You are not going to feel content or complete at the end of the day.

This is because something is lacking, something is missing. If you decide it's no longer going to affect you, that in itself is a decision. It makes it okay. What would it take to commit? Decide to do one thing in each of those low areas that moves it up one point. Would it take a lot? When you answer don't say, "There are some things that I might be able to do." The word "might" is open to non-commitment.

The words "I am" and "I will" are very powerful. You don't have to be attached to the "how" of getting there. Just say "I am going to be more fulfilled." Your intention has so much power.

Intentions

When deciding an intention, it is more important to be committed and to believe you are worthy to receive whatever it is you need, than to be specific of the details. You do have to know what you want, but it can be a general feeling rather than a particular thing or outcome. You must be careful in how you phrase your intentions so that the results will be in your best interest.

As I said before, the "how" is not important. Once you commit to the intention, the how generally becomes clear. For example, you can commit to having a travel fund. You do not need to know how much money will be in it, or where you will travel. Just decide your intention is to travel. A decision around an intention creates clarity. It is okay to be in process.

Sometimes we think we need other people's approval to fulfill our needs. This happens a lot with spouses and family members. We feel we need to discuss something we want with another person before we can take action. If that is the case, then we haven't truly committed to our intention. While input from others may be valuable, and even desired, our approval is the only approval we require.

Let's say you're going to decide to avoid a certain food. You can choose to have that food sometimes. This may be better than total denial. You can choose not to desire that food most of the time. If someone serves it to you, you can decide exactly how much you want. You approve your actions.

Stay true to your intentions. Have integrity with them. If you have a bank account in which you are saving for a vacation, then use that money for travel. Do not use it for other activities. Use it for travel, even if you spend it on gas. Use it only for its intention. If you don't use it, it will not grow. It will fall away, like a muscle. Intention grows with use.

Decide the intention when you create something. Decide and commit and then implement it. Decide its importance. Decide its value. Decisions have to be made or nothing will come of your desire. The thought will be gone. You keep the thought, incubate it and create it. You create it as part of your reality and you commit to bringing it to life.

I knew that on my fortieth birthday I didn't want a party, I wanted to wake up on a beach. I decided I wanted to wake up in St. Thomas on Sapphire Island on my birthday. My husband said, "We can't afford a trip to St. Thomas. We can't do that thing." And I said, "I have five years. I don't care how it's going to happen. I'm going to do it." That was my intention. I decided that I would go on vacation. I was going to wake up on the beach.

About six months before my fortieth birthday, I was determined that I was going to St. Thomas and my husband was convinced that we could not go. He reminded me that I was quitting my job and starting my Center and had a lot going on. He believed we could not afford a trip and were not going to make it happen. Frustrated that he had had five years to make it happen, and not feeling very important, I told him that he was not going to steal my thunder. I said, "I don't know how I'm going to be there, but I'm going to be there."

About four months before my birthday, I went to him and gave him the itinerary for the trip. I had not bought the tickets yet, but that wasn't important. I showed him the flight information, the price of the tickets, and where I would be staying. I told him that's where I will be if he wished to join me.

"You're really going without me?" he asked. I said, "I am really going to wake up on the beach on my birthday."

I had set my intention. I knew in my heart that the money would come. I did research and found a catamaran cruise that would take me not only to St.

Thomas but the rest of the Virgin Islands as well. I told him he was very welcome to come along if he could figure out a way to go. And yes, he did join me. I woke up on the beach on my birthday exactly as I had intended!

Intentions are extremely powerful, and not simply our own. We can be influenced by the intentions of others, whether good or bad. For example, if someone ties an imaginary string around your fingers it may be difficult for you to pull them apart. This is due to the power of intention. The person tying the string is using intention and making a suggestion which you believe.

Advertisements use this technique all the time. Sales people and politicians do too. Think about the media, internet, art, and entertainment. Anytime there is public discourse there is some intention behind it. Anytime someone speaks with you in private there is an intention.

You can either own it or send it back. You can block yourself from it or you can take it in and change it internally. The energy of others' intentions is real but we can change our reaction to it or what we do with it. We can be empowered.

Empowerment

When I use the word empowerment, I mean developing personal power or your internal force. This is energy we can put into anything we do, and who we become. Power, in this sense, is not power over someone, as in manipulation. It is rather an ongoing process of becoming more of who you truly are.

Empowerment means more than personal growth. It is the ability to achieve, take control of, and take responsibility for, everything in your life. It means success and living your truth.

When we are empowered, negative people do not affect us. They do not knock us off balance. Empowerment makes it impossible to let being knocked off balance ruin our day. What we want is for our environment to keep us neutral. This means balance and harmony. It means to be composed, confident, alert, aware, calm and centered.

Being unempowered means you cannot do things for yourself and you are "kept down" all of the time. It means allowing things and circumstances to overpower you. Disempowered people are victims and they blame the belief that they cannot accomplish things or become the person they want to be on others, on circumstances, on the government, economy, their spouse, their background, etc., etc. Unempowered people make excuses.

Being unempowered may lead to stress, illness, depression, and a lack of abundance. Unempowered people feel deprived and unfulfilled. They do not experience the pride and joy of accomplishment or life's pleasures. They miss opportunities and generally have a negative attitude.

This is not to say that you are unempowered if you ask for help. We all need help from time to time to stay in our truth. You are more empowered when you are comfortable knowing when a task or situation is greater than you are prepared to handle. Have you ever seen a dragonfly flying on the back of another? Many people have the mistaken impression that the two are having a sexual encounter. But that is not the case. They do it because they fly such long distances. When one dragonfly gets tired, it rests on the back of another. It is still moving in the direction it wants to go. It is still flying, but the dragonfly's buddy gives her a bit of a break. When she gets her strength back, she goes on. Dragonflies swap roles, knowing it's okay to take assistance from one another – a lesson all of us should learn.

Dragonfly embodies a stripping away of all the

beliefs that say we cannot do this or that, achieve a dream or goal. It reminds us that anything is possible when we understand we are part of Spirit, and because of that we have the power to manifest anything we desire.

The dragonfly also teaches us how to combine emotion with rational thought. Remember they are predators eating small fish, tadpoles, and other insects. A dragonfly can help us to eat away at anything in our lives that is out of control. If you feel a lack of emotional energy or too much rationality (which could lead to detachment), then the dragonfly reminds us to let go of burdens, and fly away with total freedom – to hop, skip, jump, and dance.

In our culture, people are not encouraged to feel the wide range of emotions we have been blessed to be able to experience. Too often the energy gets trapped or stuffed down, especially in the lower chakras. Working with dragonfly energy, calling it into the lower chakras can help stir this energy up and get it moving again. To work with this, if you don't know a dragonfly person to help you through the process, simply call in the energy of dragonfly through your mind. Simply thinking about it is enough. Next, visualize the dragonfly moving through your lower chakras, infusing them with clear, brilliant colors, the most beautiful you can imagine. Feel the emotions. Cry, yell, stomp your feet, do whatever it takes to get that energy up and out. However, if you are afraid the emotions you need to clear are too strong, or are concerned you might "lose it," you should consult with a healer or therapist before beginning any healing work. It's a sign of true strength and power to know we all need help from time to time.

The dragonfly has a special way of bringing deep thoughts to the surface. These thoughts need attention because they are about to emerge into their own flight, they want to come out and manifest. It could be lessons we must learn or old thoughts and energies that must undergo a transformation of their own and become new. The dragonfly teaches us to look beyond the surface and explore the deeper places of our mind and consciousness, particularly the emotional and subconscious realms. We can use the dragonfly's energy to give shape and life to these deep thoughts in the way we desire.

When you wish to uncover these deep thoughts, you can use some simple meditation. They will take the path of the dragonfly and will crawl out of the subconscious mind, that is the water, and become available to your conscious mind, that is the air.

Simple Meditation Exercise

Close your eyes and focus on a thought or feeling. Allow this thought to rise to the surface and float. It becomes clearer and more colorful and begins to take shape. Allow it to develop its independence until it is ready to fly away on its own. This same process can be used to manifest your desires.

Sometimes when we are off balance and feeling unempowered, we change our behaviors. At this point we need to remember that it's not our behaviors that are keeping us off balance. Usually it is that we are allowing ourselves to be controlled or influenced by others or by outside forces. We allow the behaviors of others to change us.

You could be in a negative situation. You could have someone dominating you or making you feel certain ways or making you react in negative ways. Someone could be completely violating your ability to have instincts, to have your own truth, and your own feelings. That person may have their own reasoning and justification for why they are doing what they are doing, but that doesn't make it right.

You don't have to buy into their reasoning. You have your own truth. You don't have to share it with them. What sometimes happens is we think we need to convince the other person that what we are seeing, sensing, and knowing is our truth. We do this for validation, confirmation, and sometimes acceptance. But if they are causing a problem and violating us, then we don't need them on our side. Trying to get them on your side, in many cases, is a form of overcompensation. You are trying to build up your self-worth with their validation.

But what if you did nothing and you said nothing

and you just felt your truth and you knew it to be true with every ounce of your being? Then if something went wrong, you would not jump to saying, "I told you so." What you could say is, "Thank you for the awareness." Our goal here is to be empowered.

A root cause of being off balance is when we allow other energies to override our own. We become unempowered when we are acting and responding to other people or to outside forces instead of either being proactive, or doing nothing, not responding and not caring. You always have those two options. To do nothing or to act with purpose and intention. You can always fight fire with fire.

You can react in a good way and a positive light. The actions of others do not necessarily have to be okay. What has to be okay is either you decide to be okay with their actions, or you do something different. Not liking someone else's actions or a situation is not going to get you anywhere. You need to decide to care less, give up, do something about it, or do something different entirely.

Another symptom of being off balance and unempowered is we begin to feel there is something wrong with our judgment or something is wrong with us. This is not so. Some things aren't always what they seem. Often we have feelings that aren't true because of fear-based thinking and worry.

I have an agreement with one of my friends. She

knows that if I start to complain, speaking from a fear perspective, or I'm griping about something, or I'm talking negatively, she is never to say to me, "You'll be fine. You're going to be okay. Don't worry about it." She knows not to respond and say those words to me because she knows in my mind they feel dismissive to my pain and mean, "Martha, be strong. Toughen up. You are worrying over something that is no big deal. You don't need to feel like you're under stress, worried." Basically, just saying, "get over it."

I don't get this way very often, but when I do, I know me, I'm looking for somebody to understand that I'm having a disempowered moment and I'm struggling. She knows that if I say to her, "I worry, I have this situation, I don't know what I'm going to do" and on and on, she'll say, "Oh my gosh, that is so stressful. That is so hard. I don't know how you do it. It is so much. You've got so much going on right now." She matches my energy through empathy and she acknowledges me. She doesn't say anything else.

The next thing that happens is I say, "You know what, it is a lot. But you know what, if I do this or that, I'm going to be okay." Or I will think of a new way to solve the problem. I talk myself right into empowerment.

On the other hand, if my friend starts feeling disempowered and tells me about a horrible circumstance or something someone said or did that made her feel negative, I do what is right for her. Her needs are different than mine. I need someone to feel compassion for me. She needs someone to stand up for her or take her side. For her, I might begin to plot out a revenge plan (with no intention of acting it out) and that helps. She needs me to talk through it with her. I know to validate her with those feelings. I play this roll and soon she starts laughing. Sometimes the cause of her problems is her boyfriend and we come up with wild, crazy stories on how we're going to torture him for being mean to her. I might even mention I heard duct tape was on sale if she needed me to pick some up! All in fun of course.

This works for us because I know she is my safe zone and I am hers. If I try to use this process with most others, my husband for example, I do not get the same results. What happens is a lot of other people start feeling bad for you and they don't want you to feel bad so they try to fix it all. And that's not what you're looking for when you're feeling disempowered. Tough love is not the answer.

People need to be helped in different ways. People need to be talked to, healed, and loved in different ways. What works for one may not work for someone else. What disempowers one, doesn't necessarily disempower the other.

When you find someone with whom you can have this type of relationship, tell them what you need.

All you have to do is ask for what you want and help the other person learn how to give it to you. If they cannot give it to you, that's okay. It just means that for this particular need they are not the right person. You can go to other friends who might be able to help. It does not mean you end the relationship. Every situation, and every need, is different. You can talk to some people about some things, but not others. This is about getting your power back and feeling stronger. Remember we talked about the importance of the five people with who you surround yourself.

Any negative situation is just a situation. It is not going to take you down and it is not bigger than you. There is nothing out there that's bigger than you. If you respond to it or allow it to affect you and knock you off center then you feed it. You give it energy. You don't have to do that. You can protect yourself. You have the power to change it even if you have allowed it to affect you. You can turn things around and get your footing.

This is when you get back in control. You come back to your truth. You come back to your center. You come back to the path heading toward what you want. You are empowered.

Illusions

Sometimes our empowerment is clouded by illusions, whether our own, or those of others. An illusion is defined as a thing that is or is likely to be wrongly perceived or interpreted by the senses. In essence, things may not always be what they seem to be.

Often, we fall under the illusions of others. We follow the crowd rather than our gut, or our intuition, because we feel if so many people see a thing a certain way then we must be wrong. We doubt ourselves. We miss the illusion. Let me give you an example from my life. This has to do with the illusion of safety. One summer my three-year-old daughter was attending a day care where on Wednesday mornings they would take the kids for swimming lessons. For five months prior I had been having dreams about the two of us being on separate yellow or orange rafts drifting down what appeared as a very clear-water river. Amber, my daughter, would inevitably slip off. I was ahead of her and being pulled by the current and could never manage to get back. She was being pulled one way and I was being pulled another. I had to see her drowning over and over in variations of this dream. So, when the idea of her going for swimming lessons arose, I was all for it.

In addition, the school used a van to transport the children that was equipped with seat belts but they could not be used with car seats. My husband at the time was working long hours, outside in the heat, and on the night shift. Even though the other parents all felt it was safe to let their children ride in this van, I didn't. I was scared to death to let her ride in it. I just knew something was going to happen if she rode without being in a car seat. I insisted my husband Walt take Amber to the swim lessons so she wouldn't have to ride in the van. He would be tired from his shift but would still have to drag himself out of bed on Wednesday mornings to take her. I knew it was an inconvenience for him and that he didn't like it, but he did it.

One Wednesday, however, he called me at work. He told me his shift had been particularly hard and he was dead tired. He pleaded with me if he could please not take Amber that morning – could she ride the bus instead. Even though it was against my better judgement, I reluctantly agreed. As soon as I hung up every cell in my body started screaming. I began having a full-blown anxiety attack. I called him back and begged him to take her. I told him he couldn't let her ride on that bus. I didn't know why but he just couldn't. He wasn't happy but he could hear the panic in my voice, so he got out of bed and took her.

The kids used noodles to swim from one side of the pool to the other. When an instructor thought a child was ready, they would take away the noodle and watch the child as they swam across the pool. On this particular Wednesday, the day I called back to beg Walt to take her, one boy started swimming on his own. Everyone was focused on him, clapping and cheering him on. Walt looked for

Amber where the children were told to sit on the steps until it was their turn, and didn't see her. Then he noticed just the tips of what looked like her hair below the water line. He went in clothes and all and pulled her out. As he walked out of the water with her in his arms, she said something that he will never forget. "Daddy, I almost had to breathe." Walt knew from his training that the average 3-year-old could only hold their breath for about thirty seconds.

No one else at the pool had even noticed. They hadn't noticed him go into the pool and they hadn't noticed that he had pulled her out. Walt was distraught, angry, and so afraid for Amber that he left without speaking to anyone. If he hadn't been there that day, no one would have seen Amber under the water until it was too late. My dreams would have become my waking nightmare. This is how buying blindly into the illusions of others can harm you.

Other illusions are solely ours. Limitations, bad luck, failures, and problems are all illusions. With illumination, light, new information, inspiration, or a new perspective these illusions may be dispelled. Focus light and your attention directly on a negative energy or negative spirit and it will dissolve and vanish. Just like my nephew's night terrors did when he stared directly at the monsters. It may take time and repetition but it will work. Once we learn to see past them, they no longer affect us. Just as when a stage magician revels how the trick is done, we are no longer fooled by the illusion. We are empowered with the new information, with the enlightenment.

Many illusions try to keep you down. They want to keep you from becoming your true self and soaring. Some illusions are obstacles that seem like they are preventing you from your spiritual growth. The dragonfly teaches us to break through these hard shells of illusion and emerge as our true, wonderful, colorful, beautiful selves. Strip away illusions of doubt, disbelief, fear, and depression. Especially the doubt that we don't have the ability to achieve a dream or goal. Fear and doubt naturally fall away as the dragonfly energies within us emerge.

Although dragonflies have the power to see through illusions, they can also create illusions. The dragonfly's skin creates reflections and refractions of light and color. This can appear magical and can be entrancing. This is not really an illusion, it is simply their skin. However, as a symbol of creating illusions, this represents a caution not to become dazzled or astonished by one's own reflections and refractions. It means to be careful of your self-created illusions as these could misdirect others leading you to a very hollow and lonely place.

Dragonfly is the keeper of dreams, the knower within that sees all of our true potential and ability. It strips away the illusions that say to us we cannot achieve our dreams and goals, that we are not worthy or capable when in fact it is our birthright and our true power to create anything we choose.

Intuition

True empowerment means being comfortable listening to your intuition – your gut instinct. Intuition allows you to understand something immediately, without the need for conscious reasoning. It is a knowing deep in your bones. Too often we allow the reasoning or rationales of others to make us doubt our intuition.

One day, when I was still in the corporate world, I was running late. Everyone had already arrived by the time I pulled in, so the parking lot was empty. I jumped out of my car, closed the door, and as I did I closed my right, index finger in it and the door locked.

It hurts like crazy and I'm thinking I need to get the keys so I can unlock the door. I start digging through my purse to find them and I can't. I am so upset because just earlier I had said to myself, "I need to start putting my keys in the side pocket since I can never find them." I had the intuition and the knowing that I should do it but I didn't. I ignored my intuition.

Now my finger is stuck in the door and I'm starting to panic and hyperventilate because it's hurting and numb at the same time, and now I'm sure I've cut my finger off and I can't get out and there's no one around to help me or to hear me scream. At that moment I heard this man's voice in my head, a loud voice I've heard on more than one occasion, and he sternly says, "Martha, if you cut your finger off you would be able to pull it out." It shocked me to hear this voice coming from nowhere. But he said it in a way that made me stop and think. He's right of course. He brought me out of panic and my irrational thinking.

I calmed down and found my keys and unlocked the door. I went straight into the office holding my finger perfectly straight with my left hand and squeezing it. It was extremely painful. I walked directly into the Vice President of Manufacturing's office and yelled at him to get me some ice. Now, so that you know, everyone is afraid of him and I'm barking orders at him. He brings the ice and I tell him the story of how I locked my finger in the car door and that I really think I need to go to the emergency room. I ask him to take me. He said, "No, it's just your finger, it looks fine, it's not bleeding." I ask him again and again he tells me that he's not going to take me to the emergency room, that I should just give it some time.

Once more, although my intuition is telling me I need to go, I acquiesce and wait for a time. The finger continues to throb and the pain is getting worse and worse. Finally, I tell him I can't wait any longer and he has to take me because I can't drive myself. I have to keep holding my finger straight with my left hand and squeezing it to lessen the pain. He agrees to take me and starts heading toward the ER that is a mile from our company.

Something in me said *no, you can't go to that emergency room, you need to go to the one at Arrowhead.* So that's what I told him. He said he wouldn't do that, it was ten miles away. This time I was adamant and wouldn't relent until he agreed. I'm lucky he didn't fire me on the spot.

The whole way there, out loud, I'm pleading with my runners and spirit guides. I ask them to please go ahead and find us a parking spot. I'm saying, "Runners, please go get to the emergency room and clear it out so I don't have to wait." My boss is not into any of this and I can tell it's making him uncomfortable.

He drops me off to go park and I go in. Blessedly there is no one in the waiting room. They take me back and immediately a doctor comes in and says, "Today is your lucky day. I'm a hand surgeon and I'm on call here because they were short-staffed. I don't usually work in the ER." Perplexed I said, "short-staffed? There wasn't even a wait for me to be brought back." His reply was, "Are you kidding me? This is the first break I've had in 8 hours!" My boss just stared at me with wide eyes. After x-raying the finger, he said to my boss, "It's a good thing you brought her in when you did because this type of injury would kill her in a matter of hours."

I'll spare you the gory details but apparently, the way my finger had been crushed was causing the blood to pool in a bad way. I could have died from blood poisoning. I could also have lost my nail for good on that finger. But none of that happened. Because I listened to my intuition, I reaped the benefit of a hand surgeon who not only kept me alive but saved my nail as well. By the way, when we left the emergency room was packed with people.

To others my finger looked like one thing, but my intuition told me something was very wrong, and very bad. I could have allowed outside influences to tell me otherwise, particularly being in pain and not thinking straight. I could have, and that would have resulted in a whole different outcome.

Intuition is a nonconscious process that operates all the time in complex decision-making. Usually we just don't give it credit. We fall back on rationalization for our feelings and actions because it's hard to give control to something of which we aren't even aware. If we listen to our intuition, it can keep us from over-thinking a situation. It can empower us.

Superheroes

It is hard to stay in an empowered state all of the time, no matter how much we may strive to. When I feel some disempowerment in a situation, one of the things I do is imagine that I become my superhero self.

When we think of superheroes we tend to think of Superman, Spider-Man, Wonder Woman, or The Incredible Hulk. I even learned there was a Super-Heroine named Dragonfly (from Americomics 1983)! However, a superhero is someone who teaches us to be heroes ourselves, to be more than what we are, to be super-people. A superhero is somebody you can look up to and can be your mentor. In some sense, they teach us to become dragonflies!

For me, it was Jiminy Cricket who taught me to be more. He taught me how to dream about the future and not pay attention to what was going on negatively around me. He taught me how to focus on my desires. He also taught me to pay attention to my inner mind. His signature phrase, "Let your conscience be your guide," became one of my mantras. He gave me the courage to look within and determine what felt right from what felt wrong. That is why he was my superhero.

Superheroes come in all shapes, sizes, and entities. My daughter's superhero has at times been an angel. Kaylee was born prematurely. I can't know for sure if her premature birth had anything to do with it, but from the time she was born she was very sensitive. She saw, sensed, and knew things that others did not. It could be that she had simply inherited my abilities as an empath and psychic.

When Kaylee was about five-years-old, I put her into an introductory Reiki class for children to help her learn how to deal with her abilities. She didn't want to go. She was a shy child and wasn't comfortable being with people she didn't know. When she came home from class she ran into my room hysterical, excited, and wide-eyed. "Mommy, mommy, where's your angel cards? Where's your angel cards? I've got to tell you something!" she yelled. I handed my angel deck to her and she started furiously going through the cards. Finally, she picked one up and gave it to me. "It's her, it's her!" she said. "What is her?" I asked. "I was so scared, and I was standing there, and this is the angel. She pushed me. I was just standing there. I didn't want to go up and do my Reiki in front of the class. She came up behind me and she pushed me and I went falling forward. When I did, I just felt okay. I wasn't scared anymore. And I did it."

When I looked at the card, I saw it was the angel of safety and security. There is no way Kaylee would have known that since her reading comprehension wasn't mature enough at five. She had seen this angel in her class, and continued to look to this angel as her superhero whenever she needed a little extra courage.

Who is your superhero? For some of you it could be a character from comic books or a cartoon character. It could be someone from classic literature or mythology. It could be a friend, teacher, or boss you admire. I invite you to look back over your life, especially between the ages of one and fourteen and just think of what and who inspired you. What character did you love to read or watch?

Here are some examples of my clients' Superheroes and why they choose them:

Tweety Bird – because he always has a positive outlook yet teases the cat. He is ornery, small and mighty.

Princess Leia – because she takes charge. She is willing to fight for what she believes.

Woody Woodpecker – because he doesn't care what other people think of him. He does his own thing.

Tinkerbell – because she has a playful attitude and can fly. She is determined to get what she wants.

Gilgamesh – because he shows the path of accomplishing great deeds.

Kermit the Frog – because of his leadership and always doing the right thing.

Batman – because of his deductive reasoning and gadgeteering knowledge.

Dr. Strange – because of his deep knowledge and abilities in magic and therefore, great spiritual connection.

Superheroes are people or characters that have traits which we aspire to have. The interesting point is, it's not that we are aspiring to them. It's that we already possess them or we wouldn't resonate with them. These are your character traits. They are traits that you value because they are a part of who you are.

A lot of times we worship things outside of us, but it's really just a reflection. For example, we may worship role models or mentors. We may highly revere people in positions that we would aspire to have. Many times, we feel jealous of things we don't have because we have a desire to have what another has. Instead of being jealous we can switch our jealousies into envies. This completely shifts the energy. If you're jealous of somebody, what are you jealous of? They possess something you wish you had. The reason you wish you had it is not because you lack it, it's just because you haven't stepped up and owned it as your truth. It is because you have not decided it was safe enough to have it. To be it. To allow it.

It took me a long, long time to allow my inner Jiminy Cricket to come out. It took a long time to be able to be someone who is not afraid to be heard, to state my opinions freely, and yes, sometimes to annoy people. Sometimes, especially in my workshops, my inner Jiminy Cricket is the one that tells me to stand up, be positive, and encourages me to take the right action. He says do the right thing, be aware before deciding, and before doing anything, think.

Looking back, as I got older and more in tune with my life's purposes of being a Transformational Life Coach, Spiritual Counselor, and Hypnotherapist, it dawned on me that I had a new superhero as a young adult. Rafiki! Do you remember him from the Lion King movie?

Rafiki's Personality from Disney's Wikia

"Rafiki is extremely sagacious and wise. His way of exploiting his intelligence, however, is highly irregular; he prefers to teach his pupils (such as Simba) by bombarding them with cryptic metaphors, and typically in a way that purposely annoys them. He takes great joy in this, and although unconventional, the methods of his teaching have proven to be effective time and time again. It should be noted that part of the reason Rafiki's teachings are rather eccentric is the fact that

Rafiki, himself, is fairly eccentric. He is excitable, energetic in spite of his age, and tends to fall into fits of hysterical laughter when something amuses him. He also tends to speak in third-person when speaking of himself.

Nevertheless, Rafiki does have a tamer side. He takes his role as the sage of the Pride Lands somberly and will act diligently to ensure the balance of "The Circle of Life" remains intact. He is also deeply connected to the spiritual world."

You may or may not know this, but a lot of the work hypnotherapists do with the subconscious mind is through metaphor. This is the perfect example of the mirror I spoke of earlier. I resonate with Rafiki because deep down inside he reflects the traits I aspire to have both personally and professionally.

One of my favorite parts is the scene where Rafiki and Simba are talking about facing his past and Rafiki whacks Simba on the head with his walking stick. Simba says, "Ouch, geez what was that for?" and Rafiki says, "it does not matter, it was in the past," and Simba replies, "yeah, but it still hurts." Then Rafiki says, "Yes, the past can hurt. But the way I see it, you can either run from it or learn from it, so what are you going to do?"

This is the ultimate Rafiki tidbit. It really sums up all of his wisdom. Bad things happen, learn what you can and keep moving forward.

When we are in our superhero self we are happy. We are emotionally satisfied. We are non-indulgent with alcohol, or food, or drugs, or behaviors because we are fulfilled. It doesn't mean you can't have a little bit but you don't indulge to excess. Inside your Superhero-self you are creative. You are generous. You're not coming from a lack mentality. You are happy and you want to share this with everyone. You want to show off your playful dance.

Want to have a little fun? Let's draw your superhero self.

Superhero Exercise

Get out some paper and crayons and get drawing your superhero self. This is a drawing of you as your superhero. It is your version of that character. Give your superhero a name. This is who you really want to be. Who are you inside when nobody else is looking? What if nobody had any judgement or cared, who would you be? How would you be showing up in the world? Imagine yourself with your shoulders pulled back and chest out. Would you have a cape and a tiara? Would you have a sword and shield? Do you have an animal companion? Would you rule the world? Would you have an army of servants? What would you have? What would you do? What would you be? What if you possessed every character trait you ever wanted? What would that look like?

Let's try a little visualization exercise. Something that you imagine or visualize is just as real as an invisible radio transmission, because the frequency is real. A thought transmits a frequency. It has space and energy. Everything has a frequency and emits a vibration. There are so many different frequencies around us. But, we have the ability to shift our frequency. Doing the exercises in this book will have a colossal effect on your ability to make shifts at will.

The mirror visualization is a simple but powerful way to create a shield or force field of protection around you. It is a way to block negative energy. You can use this when you start your day or during any situation, especially if you find yourself in a negative environment. You simply visualize putting mirrors around you.

Mirror Exercise

Stand and pivot around in a circle while projecting with your mind and imagination several mirrors, with the reflective side facing out. These mirrors form walls around you. They could even be one cylindrical mirror or even a sphere. This is a wall of protection. Anything negative or undesired gets reflected off the mirrors. The things reflected do not necessarily have to be negative, they could simply be things that are not in harmony with what you want at this time, or they are things that do not resonate with you. They could be thoughts, emotions, people, circumstances, or any other type of energy. As you create these mirrors see also a warm white light growing within you. This is your center and source and it is cleansing out anything which does not belong from your space.

The mirrors can also allow in what you want. If someone sends something good at you then you want to receive it. You can also send something good in return. If someone sends something bad at you, the mirrors reflect it and you do not choose to take it on. Anything anyone sends to you, it is always your choice to accept or reject it.

When I see or feel a bad attitude approaching, I think of Wonder Woman and her metal wrist bands that can deflect bullets. I imagine I'm wearing those bands and they deflect negative energy. I even hear the *ting! ting! ting!* sound effects.

Remember, we can say "No. Thank you." We have the ability to return to sender. If we choose to have a bad attitude then who's problem is it? It is ours, we have to own it because we allowed it in.

Love Languages

The Heart chakra is one of the most important centers of energy in our body. If you recall, part of that energy is the right to love and be loved. We want people to love us the way we want to be loved. We, in turn, love others the way we want to be loved because our natural default is to do what we would want. The problem with this is that it is a self-centered approach. Rarely does the person you are loving have the same love language as you.

The Love Languages are the ways in which people express and receive love. The term was coined by Gary Chapman in his book *The Five Love Languages.* If you haven't had a chance to read it, I would highly recommend you do. The idea is that since we have different personalities and different ways of communicating, it stands to reason we would have different ways of experiencing, giving, and receiving love. To have deep and meaningful relationships he encourages us not to use the love language that you prefer, but the one your loved one will receive best.

The five love languages are: Words of Affirmation, Acts of Service, Receiving Gifts, Quality Time, and Personal Touch. Mr. Chapman believes we all have a primary and a secondary love language. When we take the time to see things through our loved one's eyes, we can become more thoughtful and intentional about how we love them.

This means if you are loving them the way you want to be loved, they are not being loved the way they want to be loved. You have created a disconnection. Someone could say, "I'm doing everything for you," and that may be true for that person. But, the one receiving doesn't see it like that because it wasn't done in a way that felt fulfilling for them. It wasn't done in the right love language. The person receiving might respond with, "You haven't done anything for me." Does this sound familiar?

If a woman tries to love her husband through physical touch and words of affirmation when those are not his love languages, then he would not receive her love. It may appear as if he didn't care. The more she does, the more distant he gets. If we love people the way they want to be loved and love them for the way they are and who they are, they in turn will love us for who we are.

Understanding the love language of another is not always easy. Sometimes you can do it through intentional observation. If you see a loved one constantly handing out gifts, then you might safely assume that one of their love languages, perhaps

even their primary language, is receiving gifts. To be loving to this person means you need to express that love by giving them gifts. It wouldn't necessarily need to be physical gifts either. It could be a gift of time by offering to babysit her children so she could get a pedicure.

You might observe that a loved one is constantly volunteering to help others. You might show your love for that person by volunteering along side them, or volunteering to fix something for them, or planning and delivering a meal if you know they are super-busy.

Unfortunately, when it comes to love languages, observation is rarely enough. Some of the things you observe, your loved one may be doing because they feel they "have to" rather than because this is truly the way they like to receive love. Communication is the only sure way to understand how another wants to be loved.

Effectively communicating means knowing first exactly how it is that you wish to receive love and be loved. Set some time aside to think about and answer the following questions. It may help to have a few people in mind whose love you cherish or want more of.

1. What ways do you want people to show their love and appreciation for you?
2. In what ways are you most hurt or disappointed by others who you want to love and

appreciate you? What is lacking?

3. How do you show your love and appreciation to others?

4. What have you observed regarding how you show your love and appreciation to others that affects them? Are they happy? Are they distant? Are they unappreciative?

Once you are clear on your love languages, you can begin a conversation. Choose someone you identified who doesn't give love in the language that you prefer. Let them know that you understand they are trying to love you and you appreciate them for that. Then let them in on the secrets that would truly make you feel cherished. Ask them in return how you could best love them. It may take a bit of education and maybe more than one conversation, but when done with the intention of deepening love it will bring greater joy and happiness into both your lives.

Here is an exercise you can do to clear your Heart chakra to ensure your ability to love and be loved.

Clear the Heart Chakra Exercise

Close your eyes. Place your attention on your Heart chakra, right in the middle of your chest. Breathe into it. Allow yourself to connect to your Heart chakra, take a moment to just notice what this green chakra feels or maybe looks like.

Allow yourself to become aware of the blocks or information it contains. Allow any communications or insights to flood into your mind. Repeat with me, *Divine Healing Energy, I ask you to open my Heart chakra. Fill my heart with healing energy, so much so it flows over and pumps through my entire being, releasing any unforgiveness, any stress, loneliness, hatred, resentment, grief, sorrow, or anger. Melt away any sickness, any hardness, coldness, hurt, and protection that I carry in my heart. If I experience any relationship problems, both internally and externally, bring them to the surface and begin healing them. If I carry protective armor around my heart, please destroy it so my heart can breathe, so my heart can sing, dance, laugh, and love.*

Imagine that you could open your heart and look into it. Allow what you see and feel to come to your awareness. Is the door to your heart wide open and welcoming or shut with a lock on it? If the door is wide open, allow your heart to rejoice, becoming aware of all the wonderful people that love you and everything you have to be grateful for in life. If the door to your heart is locked, then allow yourself to find the place where you've hidden the key. Once you've found the place, take the key and unlock the door. Because the door has been shut, you may have to spend some time tidying up. Imagine yourself washing your heart like you would wash the most precious jewel. Remember your heart is priceless to you. Because no matter how you've treated it, it still keeps beating. This is your opportunity to show it the love and affection it needs.

When you've washed the heart, place your hands over your heart and ask if it has a message for you. When you've received a message your Divine Spirit hands you a big green diamond. This diamond represents your strength, courage, and power. Allow yourself to receive it.

You take the diamond and you place it into your heart. Allowing the beautiful green energy to melt away all fear, pain, and anxiety, and transform it into softness, gentleness, and love. You begin to see the world and yourself differently. You recognize what you thought were your mistakes were your opportunities. You begin to feel like you can welcome amazing people and incredible experiences into your life and that you're worthy of having them.

Now repeat with me, *I now choose to accept wonderful healing and loving energy into my life and have reawakened my heart and passion for life. I now allow myself to have wonderful relationships with others and attract loving people in to my life.*

When you are ready, allow yourself to begin coming back and open your eyes.

Homeopathy

Homeopathy is based on the concept of like cures like, which in turn is based on the Law of Similarities. This law has to do with frequencies and matching energies, meaning that if something is similar enough it can create healing. Think of it like how an opera singer can shatter a glass by matching the frequency of the glass. This ability of the singer has been recreated in labs with equipment many times. The adage, fighting fire with fire, is the embodiment of homeopathy. It is a phrase I often use when I teach my classes; "We're going to be fighting fire with fire and winging it." Don't forget, we are dragonflies, so we wing it.

Homeopathy was created by Samuel Hahnemann in 1796. It is based on and works by vibration. This means that a remedy that produces symptoms in a healthy person will cure those same symptoms when manifested by a person in a diseased state. Since that time, this law of cure has been verified by millions of homoeopaths all over the world. Hahnemann would dilute a substance and then use a process called succussion. Succussion means to shake the solution a number of times against an elastic body. That solution could then be diluted once again and succussed again. This process could be repeated several times until the original substance was virtually gone, but the vibration remained. In fact, the potency increased with each succussion.

Hahnemann also developed the concept of *miasms*, which are the underlying infectious principles of a disease. In other words, a miasm is a prime energy pattern that causes the illness or disease. The key words here are energy pattern. Miasms can be suppressed or masked by medicines and other superficial treatments. When this happens the miasm simply turns deeper into the body and may attach to internal organs causing more problems. The miasm produces a disruption of the flow of life force, energy, in the body. The original miasm must be treated, rather than treating only the outward symptom.

Miasms can be attracted by negative emotions and mental states. A person who has a negative attitude will tend to have a weaker immune system and also be more susceptible to disease. Negative emotions vibrate at a lower frequency and have lower energy. That is why they cannot ward off disease as easily.

Homeopathic Remedies

As you may recall, I became interested in homeopathic remedies when I was trying to help my dog to heal. I spent years studying and continue to study the unique ways the body has of healing itself. Just as with traditional western medicine, homeopathy is continually evolving. Please understand, I am not in any way implying that homeopathy is the be all and end all. There are legitimate times when western medicine is totally appropriate and necessary. They can be perfect partners which I will explain later in the story of how I beat thyroid cancer.

When prescribing remedies, homeopathic practitioners use two types of reference sources. The first reference is called a *materia medica*. Materia media are Latin words that mean "materials of medicine." Homeopathic medicines are listed in Latin so that homeopaths (and patients) can be precise with the exact source of the medicinal substance. There are many different types of materia medica but each is a collection of pictures of drugs or medicines organized by remedy, with the symptoms the remedy is designed to treat listed.

The second reference is a homeopathic repertory. A repertory is simply defined as a place where something can be found. This is an index of symptoms first, with the associated remedies for those specific symptoms.

The remedies can be made of a wide variety of

substances including plants, animals, minerals, and even synthetics. Sometimes venom or other poisons are used. However, in homeopathy, these are not harmful. Hormones and other secretions can be used. In some cases, waste material, blood, or other tissue can be used.

More recently, a class of remedies called "imponderables" has generated much interest among homeopaths. Imponderables do not come from a substance. They come from electromagnetic energy that has been captured by either alcohol or lactose. These energies could be ultraviolet rays, radio waves, X-rays, Gamma rays, and many more.

Homeopathic remedies are usually taken in the form of droplets or pills. New methods and treatments are always being tested and developed as homeopathy continues to gain popularity.

Here's an interesting question. What do a red onion, a flu bug, and arsenic have in common? They are like energies. One homeopathic remedy is Allium Cepa. The onion is the most widely cultivated genus of Allium. When we take Allium Cepa at the onset of the first signal that there is a problem it acts like an army. It is especially great for allergies. It begins shedding the problem and this allows the body to start self-recovery. Allium Cepa comes to the rescue by giving the body a boost of power. It fights fire with fire.

Homeopathic medicine works by using the same

energy of the problem to nullify the problem. Therefore, the problem cannot continue to be created because it's not even there. If you take a remedy at the onset, then your body has not yet been taken over by the problem. The key to using homeopathy successfully is to catch it quickly, match the symptoms, and be proactive. It's important to take homeopathic remedies early on so your body's immune system is not weak.

Supplements can help but they take time. You have to allow time for digestion and absorption. This process also takes energy. This is why taking the homeopathics right away, while your body still has its own force, is very helpful.

If you had a red onion in front of you and you cut this onion and the juice flies up, what happens? Your eyes water, your nose runs, your eyes burn. What's happening in your body when your eyes are responding like this? Your body naturally responds to the foreign energy and it works to get rid of it. The eyes and nose run so the energy can clear out.

If your eyes and nose run when there is no red onion around, you may think it's just allergies, a cold, or maybe it's the beginning of the flu. You would not instantly think you were deathly ill. You would know that it's just the onset of something and that is a signal to do something about it.

The essence of red onion acts as an aide to the body.

When your body is in release mode, it is doing what it is designed to do. We are taught to take a Sudafed or a Claritin or some cold medicine when we want the drainage to stop. What happens when we stop the drainage reaction? We put up an imaginary blind that says "you can't see me" and this hides the reaction. The underlying sickness is hitting this imaginary wall. All medications do this. It doesn't matter if it's thyroid, or antidepressants, or stomach medication. They do not create what your body wants. Your body is screaming inside you that you're only masking the real issue, but you do not hear it.

This is like driving down the road, having your check engine light come on, and the way you deal with it is to get a Band Aid, cover up the light and keep driving. Sometimes we think that covering it up makes it better. But, what if the check engine light came on because there was a loose speaker wire, or something simple? If this were the case, then the fact that you keep driving doesn't matter because the problem won't hurt you. You just won't have any music when it breaks. But if it is your radiator hose, then that is a bigger problem and you will not be able to get very far. In this case the Band Aid did not do anything but gain you a few feet or miles. Now you've potentially blown up your whole engine by ignoring it. The same is true for us. It is true for our bodies, minds, and spirits.

There are other ways to cure a dis-ease or problem

homeopathically. All one needs to do is match the frequency to blow out and destroy the original negative energy that caused the dis-ease. This can be done mentally or emotionally.

Matching the Energy

The Matching the Energy technique is done using both the mind and the emotions. Let's say you have a negative circumstance. You consciously match the energy of the situation with the same emotional energy. You use this emotional energy to blast away the negative thing. For example, if someone is criticizing you, you can easily match their energy. You can still be polite to them while at the same time giving them back their own frequency; returning it to sender. Then they have nowhere to go. You come back at them with the same energy and this neutralizes them.

I promised you my personal story of blending homeopathy and western medicine to deal with my diagnosis of thyroid cancer. It seems appropriate to share it here. In this case, as you will see, I used surgery and emotional energy to match the energy of my disease.

After working in the corporate world for some time, and hating every minute of it, I started having problems. I kept getting nauseous. It only happened when I turned my head a certain way. I kept wondering, "What is this about?" I'd never had this consistent feeling of nausea and it made no sense to me. It went on for a few months until one day I felt truly sick. There was a weird feeling on my neck and it kept bugging me. Something kept drawing my attention to it even though there was never any pain. It continued to grow until at one point I realized there was something there.

I went to the doctor to have it checked out. They sent me to an oncologist who did a biopsy. Low and behold, they call me in and they say, "Martha, we hate to tell you this but you've got malignant cancer of the thyroid. We're going to give you radiation in the form of a pill and try to kill it off. We will then need to do surgery. You're most likely going to have a trachea. You'll lose your voice box and at best you may, or may not, have five years to live through all of this."

Obviously, this was not good news. I had grown up with the belief that you had to follow doctor's orders. You don't ask questions, the doctor is the authority, you do what he says. But deep inside I knew that this course of treatment was absolutely wrong. I hadn't yet discovered homeopathy, I hadn't started my hypnotherapy practice, yet still I knew that this was not the total answer.

I had a big melt-down. I did not know what to do or what would happen. I wondered who was going to raise my two-year-old daughter. Who would do all the things I knew how to do? My husband? He's a great guy but I know she needs me! It was a trauma. It was huge.

I asked for a different course of treatment. They told me the only other option would be that they could go in and try to remove it, but it wasn't recommended. They reiterated that if I didn't have the radiation treatments, and even if I did, I might only have five years left. *How could this be? One day I was perfectly fine, then I feel something, and suddenly my whole life is completely different.* I still couldn't bring myself to agree.

Something inside me changed when I left the office. Rage boiled up inside me. I was so mad. All I could think about was how dare they. How dare they tell me that today I'm going to lay down and die? How dare they!? Who are they to say that I got up this morning but now my life is over and assume I'm just going to accept what they said and fall in line? Who are they?

I was in the grocery store, in the baby food aisle having all these feelings. I'm reading through all the labels or I'm trying to because that's the kind of mother I am. But I can't get my mind off the fact of who is going to do this for my child? Who is going to read the labels and make sure that she gets what she needs? In the middle of these sad, stressful thoughts I feel a tap on my shoulder. This older woman had walked up beside me. She wagged her finger at me and said, "Honey, you can either believe you've got it or you can believe you don't. You need to make a choice and make a good one."

I stood there, completely stunned – no thoughts, no emotions. I wondered if she had read my mind. I was so caught off guard having been immersed in my head and myself. Then I looked around and there was no lady to be seen. She was nowhere in sight. Had she even been real? Her words though, reminded me of me, and who I was, and what I believed.

I lost it all in that moment. I had nobody to empower me. Nobody to help me out of the seemingly impossible options and say you can do this instead. Everyone around me was grieving as I was. The lady's words infuriated me. Not at her for having said them, but at the medical professionals. She was right. I was the one who had to choose, not them. Who were they to tell me I'm going to die and someone else is going to raise my child?

I left the grocery store. I was so angry I don't even know what I did with my cart. I drove home in a fury, tires screeching. I was so angry and livid. I stormed into my house having the fit of a lifetime. I went into the bathroom shouting. My husband, who was forced to witness all this, was completely bewildered wondering if I'd lost my mind. All he knew was I just got back from the grocery store and had somehow transformed into a beast. I was saying the same things as before, "How dare they! How dare they tell me that today is the last day of the rest of my life! How dare they tell me that somebody else is going to raise my kid! How dare they tell me that I was fine yesterday but now my life is over! Who are they? Are they God? I will not take chemotherapy. I am not going to be put in some basement, given some radiation pill, and have to stay down there and not be around anybody. I am not going to lose my hair. I'm not going to be on medication the rest of my life. I'm not going to do any of that. I'm not going to do it. They can forget about it. I am not going to let them tell me that's my fate!" I got mad, very mad.

My husband suggested we talk about it. He was scared for good reason. He thought I was going to die, and that I was refusing help. But something in me was so strong. It was so powerful and intense, like a warrior spirit. I really got a rush that day. To this day, I am able to conjure that energy and use it to make a decision.

What I learned later on, was that the thyroid sits in the Throat chakra. The Throat chakra is all about suppressed emotions, things we haven't said, things we should have said, and things we shouldn't have said. Everything that we've swallowed, all that energy resides there. The blue center of the chakra becomes very suppressed when we swallow everything and growths begin to form from the things that want to come out of you. I believe in my rage, in my yelling fit, I was blowing out my Throat chakra and releasing all of that energy that was bottled up and cocooned there in the form of a tumor.

I became enraged and angry – I became red, the opposite of the blue of the Throat chakra. I was using fire energy to combat an excess of water energy.

I finally decided to let the doctors take it out. But, I gave them strict orders only to take out the side where it was and not the other side, and not to do anything else! I still refused to do any kind of radiation treatment. So, they did the surgery expecting the worse. Almost five hours later, for a surgery they said would only take 45 to 90 minutes the doctor came out and announced to my family that I didn't have cancer. He said, "We just don't understand. The preliminary tests are saying there's no cancer. But I have to warn you. We need to send the mass to the lab and in five days, we're pretty sure they're going to send it back confirming that it is cancerous, and we're going to have to go back in and remove the rest of it."

They had done a lot of extensive work during the surgery because the tumor had grown through my ligaments and wrapped around back behind my neck. But they still couldn't figure out why it wasn't testing as cancer. They said their preliminary test had to be wrong. They said they couldn't do anything more because of the false reading and had sewn me back up. They said I'd have to return when the correct report came back from the lab in five days and they would do everything all over.

At the end of the five days, the test came back and

it still said it was not cancerous, even though all the biopsies said it was. I knew why. It was because I had released it. It was originally a throat problem and I used my communication to blow it out. In this case I was enraged, but it doesn't have to be done in anger. You just match the energy. What boiled up inside of me was the unexpressed energy that created the tumor to begin with.

It's such a blessing to be doing what I do and to understand now fully how I was able to help heal myself. It's been eighteen years since my surgery and I've never had a problem since. I have not had more surgery nor any medication even though they insisted I would be on medication for the rest of my life, having only one lobe functioning.

We have the power to create, good or bad. If we have a dis-ease or dysfunction in our body, on some level it began as emotional energy. We felt some way. We kept feeling that way for so long it grew strong and became our truth. Then it took a physical form. It began to have a life of its own.

I believe that everything that was created, the cancer in my throat and my closed Throat chakra, was a product of my inability to speak up. To be heard. To listen. To speak my truth. Holding back the mean things that I could say, as well as the positive. I believe I created the tumor.

When I got mad I think that I got mad about every doctor that I felt ruined my life. Every mean thing that somebody said to me. I think that I got mad and so enraged because of all of that, which is what saved my life. The very thing that created it was the very thing that corrected it. That's homeopathics!

When I blew it out, I took its power away. I no longer had to own that energy. In homeopathy, like cures like. The similarity of what created it in suppression, is the very thing that came out in expression. There is always an excess and an insufficiency when we have dis-ease in our body. It's the pendulum. We all have the power to heal within us. I am living proof.

Onward and Upward

O ne of my workshop participants asked me, "How do you get on course if you don't really know what your ultimate course is?"

My answer was, "Who cares? It's not important to know what your ultimate course is. What matters is you have a desired goal. The next question is how do you want to feel, then what would it take to start working toward that today? If you don't know where you are going then it doesn't matter where you end up. If you have no desired destination, then any path will do. If you don't have any desired outcome, then exactly what you are is fine. If you don't want to be happy, then don't. If you don't want to be sad, then don't."

The key to all of this being in or out of balance, this use of energy, is that you decide how you want to feel and where you want to be. The course and the path unfold naturally as we move along them. It's more about following a feeling and not any particular path. What you want to feel is more alive. You want to feel that you have purpose and that you are heading toward a purpose, whatever or however that looks to you. It really is all about the journey.

Your purpose will have a feeling associated with it. It is that feeling that we truly desire. For example, if you want to feel happy, then happiness is your prime goal. Every day you say, "Just for today I'm going to be happy and I'm going to follow whatever comes that leads me to happiness. I'm not going to settle for anything less." As long as you stay true to your intention, whatever comes up will never be wrong as long as it is feeding your spirit.

There is the spiritual self and there is the physical self. You can have happiness in both. You can coexist in that space. You are a spiritual being having a human experience. Spirit will lead you wherever your heart desires. Follow Spirit and listen to where it guides you.

I have a personal belief that there is already a preset place for myself in this world, a calling, and a need and a spot for my work. Each day my job is to aspire to be whatever that preset is and keep heading towards it. I do this by allowing myself to be guided and nudged and pushed by Spirit and then following.

I might end up experiencing something seemingly terrible. I might get in a car accident. I wanted to go somewhere with this great intention and I got hit in the rear-end. This is not a very positive experience for me. But if I know clearly where I was going and what my intention was, then whatever might happen in my path, good or bad, was also a part of my process, a part of my plan, a part of my journey.

It is very easy to make this intention. This is the intention to be guided by Spirit and to follow your path. This is your true path and both your physical and spiritual sides are aligned with it. Sometimes things that seem like they do not belong on the path are lessons or tests. Sometimes these things benefit us in ways we do not know or understand at first. They can teach us and help us grow.

A "bad" situation does not have to be seen as bad. It can be seen for what it is and always be changed into a positive experience. Call it a blessing in disguise. I can look at the car accident and think it just ruined my day or I can look at why did that happen for me? Do you see I said "for" me and not "to" me? How did I create this and why? I can go into a state of wonder. I wonder why I needed to be rear-ended today?

We create our realities in our thoughts and actions. Therefore, on some level, I created that crash. Maybe it meant I need to slow down or to pay attention. Maybe I did not really want to go where I was going. Maybe something tragic or strange was going to happen down the road and this accident just saved my life.

You could analyze the situation and possible lessons to death or you could simply acknowledge what happened and realize that your goal today was to remain happy. It is okay that this thing happened and you can feel thankful that you are alive and not hurt. The point is, wherever you go there you are. Why not make the best of it?

No matter what negative situations, circumstances, events, people, or problems you may be experiencing now or in the past, it is possible to empower yourself and transform into a truly beautiful being. But it isn't always easy to do it on your own. Attending workshops, or working directly with someone like me, can give you dramatic results without the frustration of trial and error that you might experience in going it alone. I have personally witnessed my clients and workshop attendees make glorious transformations, many seemingly miraculous.

I have been through so much, even when the actual circumstance hasn't happened directly to me. As an empath, one of the things I have the ability to do is process pain, the pain of others. That does not mean I have not had my own struggles or not had to deal with a lot. It does not mean that I do not have work to do. What it does mean is there are not a lot of people who I do not understand. We have all had pain. Pain is pain. The key thing to remember is that pain is inevitable, but suffering is optional. Listen and pay close attention to that again: pain is inevitable, suffering is optional.

Even after all of these negative experiences, whether my own or empathically through others, I have been able to change my life into an extremely positive and magical experience using the knowledge and principles I have shared in this book and that I teach in my programs.

You can too. You can emerge from the dark, dank waters and leave your crusty, old shell behind. You can spread your wings and fly knowing that you are perfectly in balance mentally, emotionally, physically, and spiritually. You can wear your brilliance for all to see. You can be a dragonfly. Light and free!

Meet Doctor Martha

Hello. I am Dr. Martha Reed. I am a metaphysician and spiritual counselor, life coach, empath, hypnotherapist, and healer. I am an international speaker and author. I am a mother. Above all else I am, like you, a spiritual and energy being living in this dual reality.

I hold a Ph.D. in Holistic Life Counseling from the University of Sedona, a school that emphasizes the study and application of several disciplines in the areas of metaphysics, philosophy, mysticism, and religion just to name a few.

I have been working with people to empower them with the insight to manifest their goals and desires for many years. I love connecting people with their deeper, intuitive selves while providing them with an integrative approach to make empowering and enhancing changes in their lives. Together, we create powerful, life-changing transformations.

I use a variety of proven holistic methods, healing modalities, and professional coaching practices. I believe that the power to heal and shift lies within. I take my clients inward through guidance, support, and visionary insight, and bring them to a place of mental, emotional, physical, and spiritual healing.

Throughout my life I have overcome many fears and limiting behaviors. I began making empowering changes in my life. I fully embraced my intuitive gift as a psychic medium and left a very successful twenty-year career in Corporate America to pursue my dream of opening a wellness center. This center currently thrives in Glendale, Arizona and people like you are helped every day.

Many people thought I was crazy for leaving a secure career in the middle of an economic recession. I secretly thought I was crazy too, but the leap forward, although scary, was one of the best decisions of my life. I became an international speaker, workshop leader, and author. I have written three books and co-authored two others. I have created six hypnosis audio meditations, a self-help hypnosis app, and opened both a holistic center for wellness and a salt float therapy spa.

If you would like to contact me to see how I might help you overcome the shadow side of life and learn to live in the Light, emerging into the beautiful, amazing person you were born to be, you may do so at:

admin@insightsforlife.center

Or to learn more about my workshops and events or to book a private appointment with me, visit my website at:

www.insightsforlife.center

Self-help CDs by Martha Reed
Available on Amazon

www.amazon.com/Hypno-Reiki-Clearing-Cleansing-Chakras-Martha/dp/B00F6O5N2A

www.amazon.com/Daydream-Mental-Vacation-Unwind-Hypnosis/dp/B004IH8FAS

www.amazon.com/Forever-Thin-Self-Hypnosis/dp/B003MC4YT6

www.amazon.com/Life-Energy-Martha-Reed-
PhD/dp/B004IAMD6C

www.amazon.com/Tranquility-Hypnosis-Deep-
Relaxation/dp/B004IH9PDO

Download the Free Insights for Life App
to start listening to hypnosis audios!

The FREE app, from Google Play or iTunes, allows you to tap into the unlimited power of your inner mind with the soothing voice of Dr. Martha Reed. (aka the mind whisperer). These visualizations help to reduce symptoms of depression, anxiety, stress, panic, and unwanted thought processes.

This hypnosis app is designed to create instantaneous mind shifts in acute or crisis situations! Help is not always readily available the moment you need it. I want to be right there for you, if only a whisper in your ear, a reminder letting you know you are not alone and you can overcome anything you put your mind to!

Made in the USA
Coppell, TX
06 August 2020